I KNOW THE WAY?

Lynette Jackson Love

978-0-578-60640-8

Copyright © 2019
Durham, NC

Book Project Management—Start Write Publish
contact@startwriteaway.com
http://startwriteaway.com

Start Write Team

Editor: Dr. Gerald C. Simmons
Editorial Assistants: Jennifer Eiland & Kelly R. Taylor
Front/Back Cover/Book Illustration: Rainah Davis

Layout Design: Inkcept Studio

All bible quotes are from NIV unless otherwise stated.

All rights reserved.

No part of this publication may be reproduced, distributed, or transmitted in any form or by any means, including photocopying, recording, or other electronic or mechanical methods, without the prior written permission of the publisher, except in the case of brief quotations embodied in critical reviews and certain other noncommercial uses permitted by copyright law.

Dedication

To Richard Love Sr,
Richard Love Jr, & Reggie Love,
My Three Heartbeats.

To Richard Love,
my husband of 46 years, I say thank you for
walking with me on this life journey.
Because we were married at such a young age (21),
we literally grew up together through all the
bumps, bruises, and good times. Richard has been
an eyewitness to what God has done in our lives.
It has been a blessing to see his faith grow as
we have seen God cover, protect,
and bless us.

Acknowledgments

My daughter - in love:

Many thanks to my daughter - in love, Chelsea Young – Love, for her help with editing this book. I will always appreciate her encouragement and advice to find my voice.

My Mother, Aunt, and Family who showed me The Way:

The person who impacted my faith the most was my mother Elise Jackson Grant. She was God's child and had a quiet faith, but the example of her life spoke volumes. As I watched her deal with the many challenges she encountered in her life, I concluded that the source of her strength and help was indeed God. It was from her example that I learned to call on and cry out to God and came to know on a deep and personal level that He is an ever-present help.

My mother's sister, Ina J. Brown, was a rock in her Church, Greater Zion A.M.E, and in her community for over 60 years. Also, she was the pianist at that church for almost 40 years. At her funeral, the Pastor described Aunt Ina's passing as "a tree that has fallen in the community."

As I understand it, my mother and her sister Ina were following the Christian examples set by their parents John and Pauline Johnson. Those two sisters were also influenced by the Christian example of their aunts, cousins, and the women of the previous generations. Some of these women I knew, and some I did not, but I salute them for being role models for my mother and for the legacy they left, which subsequently impacted my life as well.

I come from a huge family and have a large number of cousins. Many of them are very precious to me, but the cousin who has walked the closest with me on my faith journey is my dynamic cousin, Antinetta Vanderhorst, aka "Netta." She is a prayer warrior who has prayed with and for me on many occasions, inspired me and given me much Godly advice. I learned first-hand from her about how to pray intensely for healing. I saw God answer those heartfelt cries for healing as I witnessed God heal her son Jervay from colitis and cancer.

Aunt Ina's daughter, "Peachie" Brown-Poole, was my first cousin, a best friend, and a confidante. She was also my spiritual sister, who prayed with and for me. And I with and for her on many occasions. From her struggle and subsequent death from breast cancer, I learned that while we may not want to let go of a person and desire for him or her to be healed, death is a form of healing. Peachie and I often talked about the high standard of Christian Service set by our mothers and those other women in our lives and how we struggled (and failed) to live up to their examples.

These are the people who have helped me the most to know the way.

Table of Contents

Dedication..	3
Acknowledgements...	5
Prelude...	11
Introduction..	13

Part 1:
JESUS LEAVES A ROADMAP IN THE GOSPEL OF JOHN POINTING THE WAY (JOHN 14)

1. Jesus Tells Us to Not Let Our Hearts Be Troubled and to Believe (John 14:1-4).. 23
2. Jesus is the Only Way to God and is Truth and Life (John 14:5-6).. 28
3. Jesus and God are One (John 14:7-11). 35
4. Jesus' Followers Will Do Great Works (John 14:12).. 40
5. Jesus' Name Has Power (John 14:13-14)..................... 43
6. Jesus Says That Loving Him Means Obeying Him (John 14:15, 21, 23-24). 47
7. Jesus Gives Us the Promise of the Holy Spirit Who Will Help Show Us the Way (John 14:16-20, 25-26).. 50
8. Jesus Has Given Us His Peace (John 14:27)................. 61
9. Jesus Gave Us the John 14 Roadmap 67

Part 2:
JESUS INVITES YOU TO ABIDE IN HIM AND LET HIS SPIRIT DWELL IN YOU TO SHOW YOU THE WAY (JOHN 15)... 69

1. Abide in and Remain Connected to the Vine to Find Your Purpose and Be Fruitful (John 15: 2 - 4) . 73
2. Abide With Christ On the Vine and Reflect His Character to the World (John 15:5-6,8)..................... 75
3. Abide in His Word and Pray (John 15:7, 16) 79

4.	Abide in His Love and Obey (John 15:9-11)..................	83
5.	Abide in His Love and Love Others as Jesus Commanded (John 15:12, 17)..	85
6.	Abide in Jesus' Friendship (John 15:13-15)..................	87
7.	Abide in the True Vine and Branch Out to the World (John 15:16)	88
8.	Abiding and Sanctification (John 15:1-17, 26-27)	91
9.	Abide in Christ: What Jesus Wants You to Know About Him From John 15	94
10.	Abiding in Christ: What That Looks Like - According to Him...	95
11.	Abide in Christ: What Not Abiding in Christ Looks Like	97

STUDY QUESTIONS 113
Jesus Leaves A Roadmap in the Gospel of John Pointing the Way... 113
Jesus Invites You to Abide in Him and Let His Spirit Dwell in You to Show You the Way.................. 135

Prelude

> *"Lord, we don't know where you are going, so how will we know the way?"*
> *–John 14:5*

Jesus' disciple Thomas is confused and asks Jesus, "how will we know the way?" At the time, Thomas didn't realize that he was looking at and speaking to "The Way."

If you want to know something about someone, usually the person himself or herself is the best person to give you the information. Since Jesus understood that fact, He was very intentional about pointing out the way to His Followers.

If you are feeling as if you have gotten off track, don't stay in that situation. If you are ensnared in some things that you can't seem to break free from, don't worry; there's help available. You don't have to do it on your own; there's strength, freedom, and deliverance in the Savior Who is "the Way" back. He is the Way! Come back to Him. He is waiting with open arms.

Introduction

This Book Was Written For New Believers And Saints On The Path Of Sanctification Seeking To Know "The Way."

Is God whispering in your ear, calling you to do big, overwhelming things that seem to exceed your natural abilities and possibly your imagination? As encouragement to you, let me share the process God used to get me "off the dime" to compose this book. I remember when God put in my Spirit that I was going to write this book. My reaction was, Who me?"

Surely God couldn't be talking to me. I thought that God was either talking to the wrong person or that I was hallucinating. I then came up with the following list of reasons why I couldn't, shouldn't, wouldn't write a book of any kind:

> I did not see myself as being articulate enough to pull it off.
>
> I was absolutely not self-disciplined enough to pull it off.

I had a poor memory.

I was aging and my vocabulary was decreasing. There were words I used to know and be able to easily pronounce that I now struggled to remember.

I thought what would be required was way too overwhelming.

I had never done anything like this before, not even close.

I do not like to do tedious, detailed stuff.

If I did manage to write a book, it was going to be a very short book without many pages.

Yet, God revealed to me the following reasons why through Him, and with Him, all things are possible:

He calls us to do His work, and those He calls, He equips.

He would give me the words.

He knew my weaknesses, and He was greater than any of them. Furthermore, He would give me the "godly confidence" to shore up my weaknesses.

He would change me, grow me and transform me. It was going to be a process that would evolve over time and would get me ready to do what He was calling me to do.

He taught me about the Holy Spirit, the member of the Trinity I was least familiar with and presented the greatest confusion for me. He then made me know that I would have the power of the Holy Spirit leading me and guiding me in this endeavor.

He put me on course to get involved in Bible Study Fellowship and Shepherd's Heart Ministry for 15 years of intensive, line-by-line study of His Word. He knew that he needed to build up my limited base of knowledge for me to have something to draw upon to write this book.

God doesn't want you to be lost, He wants you to know the way to Him. That is His will for your life. He sacrificed his Son's life for that purpose. And when you accept his Son as Lord and Savior, He will place his Holy Spirit within you to indwell, help, teach, and guide you. He has given us the Bible, His Holy Word, as a lamp and a light to guide us through life. He has many wonderful promises that he has covenanted to those who belong to Him. He also has given us many hard truths and warnings to keep us on course. Jesus told us that the road to God comes straight through Him and He left us a roadmap so that we will never have to be uncertain about the route or end up off course on this life's journey. Jesus wants us to know the way for ourselves, and He also wants us to then show others the way. It is my hope that this book will encourage you to embrace the ministry work of the Great Commission to which Jesus has called us.

18 | How Will I Know The Way?

Part 1:
JESUS LEAVES A ROADMAP IN THE GOSPEL OF JOHN POINTING THE WAY (JOHN 14)

> John 13:1:
> ...Jesus knew that the hour had come for him to leave this world and go to the Father. Having loved his own who were in the world, he loved them to the end.

If you want to know something about someone, usually, the person is a good source, and in all likelihood, the best source from whom to get the information. Jesus understood this and was very intentional about pointing out the Way to Himself. So, if you are seeking Jesus, I recommend that you go directly to Him in that He is the absolute best source to help you to get to know and find the way to Him.

The Romans Roadmap uses Scriptures from the Book of Romans to draw a map of God's Plan of Salvation. Christians use it as an evangelizing tool to explain the gospel message of salvation. However,

I also see another roadmap in John 14, where Jesus is responding to a direct question from one of His disciples about how to know "The Way." The question comes from someone who knows, loves, and believes in Him, yet is mighty confused about "The Way" of which Jesus speaks. Jesus responds to the question by urging the disciples to place themselves in His and God's trustworthy hands. Jesus goes on to share some very deep revelations about Himself and teaches about obedience and doing great works for His Kingdom.

The roadmap that Jesus draws for them in John 14 unveils some marvelous promises and sources of help that will ensure their journey will be victorious. In John 14-17, Jesus leaves us an amazing discourse consisting of some of the most beautiful words He ever uttered, "Red-Letter" words that are deeply beloved by believers. If you have a "Red-Letter" edition of the Bible (the words spoken by Jesus are in red print), you will see that these chapters are a figurative "sea of red." Take a minute, and thumb through John 14-17. Thomas poses the question of how to know the way, and in John 14, Jesus draws a detailed Roadmap to help us know the way to Him, and as His followers, to know the way to grow and mature in our walk with Him.

At this point in John's gospel, Jesus' ministry on earth is drawing to a close. He is on the way to the Cross. His arrest, crucifixion, and resurrection lay just ahead, and He is trying to prepare the disciples for what is about to happen. Jesus has withdrawn from the public and has gathered the disciples unto Himself in the Upper Room for some very intimate time with Him.

In the previous chapter, John 13, Jesus gives the example of humble servanthood by washing the disciples' feet. Also, He shares the last supper with the disciples, reveals that there is a traitor in their midst, predicts Peter's denial, and commands them to love one another. On top of all that, He drops a bombshell on them: He is leaving them. He's mentioned leaving before, and they haven't quite gotten it, but now His departure is imminent. These disciples in the Upper Room with Jesus have given up a lot to walk with Him: families, homes, careers. They have co-labored with Jesus in His earthly ministry and had been in the physical presence and on the ministry team with the Son of God for over three years. They were part of the world's first Christian Ministry Street Team.

When you are in the presence of Jesus, amazing and miraculous things happen, and these disciples have been eyewitnesses to many spectacular things. There is a detailed record in the gospels of the things they have seen: miracles, healings, people being set free, resurrections, etc. They have felt the love of Jesus Christ, been transformed by His love, loved Him deeply and were hardly ready to let go of Him. When the disciples hear these things from Jesus, they are puzzled, fearful, and sorrowful. In their minds, they have just received some very sad news, but that news will turn out to be the very best of news for mankind, "the good news of the Gospel of Jesus Christ."

During Jesus' earthly ministry, the world sensed that there was something very different about this Jesus. The world had seen the miracles He had performed and heard the words He had spoken. His words were divine, and He spoke those divine words in a way that pierced right through to the hearts of His listeners, zeroing in on their needs, concerns, and fears. In that Upper Room He now speaks to His disciples' fears. And Jesus is still able and willing to minister to the concerns of your heart today.

Let's begin by hanging out in John 14. Jesus has much to say in this chapter about placing our trust in Him, truth, life, power, obedience, great works, and the Holy Spirit.

1. **Jesus Tells Us to Not Let Our Hearts Be Troubled and To Believe (John 14:1-4).**

   > Jesus and God can be trusted to cover, keep and protect you (John14:1).

   Jesus knows that the Cross and unspeakable suffering lie directly before Him. But at this moment, He focuses on comforting and encouraging His dazed disciples. The words He goes on to speak to them are stunningly beautiful and are a precious gift to believers for all times. Jesus tells us to trust in God and to trust also in Him. Me and my Father "We've got you," and we are able keep you. Two of my favorite verses that speak so beautifully to God's care of us are:

   > Deut. 33:12: "Let the beloved of the Lord rest secure in him, for he shields him all day long, and the one the Lord loves rests between his shoulders."
   >
   > Psalm 68:19: "Praise be to the Lord, to God our Savior, who daily bears our burdens. 20 Our God is a God who saves."

During the 1992 Olympic Competition, the term "Dream Team" was popularized when the USA Men's Basketball Team was stacked with the top professional basketball players from the NBA. They powered their way through their Olympic opponents, winning by huge margins and capturing the Gold Medal for the USA. That team was described as the greatest sports team ever assembled and the greatest collection of basketball talent on the planet. As loaded up with talent as members of that Dream Team were, they can't even begin to compare to the ultimate Dream Team of Jesus and God. And Jesus is telling us that for those of you who belong to Me, you have the full force of Our reliable, trustworthy power keeping you.

As a believer, you have the ultimate Dream Team working on your behalf. Your Dream Team is the one who took the formless, empty, nothingness that was in the beginning, and, through the power of God's Word, spoke the whole world into being in all of its splendor and beauty. Your Dream Team consists of a Sovereign Lord Who brings the power, and rules with a mighty arm. The One who measured the waters in the hollow of His hand, and with the breadth of His hand, marked off the heavens. He held the dust of the earth in a basket and weighed the mountains on the scales and the hills in a balance. Our God is a big, awesome God. So what is it that you are dealing with that could possibly be bigger than Him?

> Isaiah 40:10-12: See, the Sovereign Lord comes with power, and he rules with a mighty arm… Who has measured the waters in the hollow of his hand, or with the breadth of his hand marked off the heavens? Who has held the dust of the earth in a basket, or weighed the mountains on the scales and the hills in a balance?

There is an Insurance Company with a very famous slogan that promises you are in good hands with them, describes themselves as the "good hands people," and offers accident forgiveness. God's hands and Jesus' hands are way more capable than any insurance company will ever be.

They are the BIG hands, ABLE hands duo. When we fall into sin, God offers us His forgiveness, and those Divine hands throw our sins into the sea of forgetfulness. God promises us that His care of us will never falter. Know that when trouble comes and rocks our world, those who believe in and belong to Jesus have a steadfast, unmovable anchor in Whom to place our trust. The storms and fires of this life, which come upon us, can overwhelm us. We must cling to Jesus and trust Him to get us through. When those storms do come, we are called to walk through them in a manner that witnesses to the world that our God is, in fact, trustworthy.

That's what these disciples will be called to do. They are about to face some very turbulent, dark days. They will watch Jesus be arrested, brutalized, and nailed to a cross. The disciples will be tested by persecution. After basking in the glow of Jesus' love, miracles, and holy words for over three years, none of them would have predicted or desired this outcome. Some of them were probably still secretly harboring wishes for themselves because they were with Jesus (Mark 10:35-45). How would their faith fare in the days ahead? Would they stay strong? Would they continue to trust in Jesus after experiencing these tests? They are about to embark on an amazing and glorious journey as they begin their ministry of evangelizing the world with the gospel of the Good News.

As they walked through the challenging days ahead, we see them remembering Jesus' words with more clarity and understanding. We see their faith grow stronger and bolder. Through the power of their risen Savior and the help of the Holy Spirit, they faced down the storms and left a marvelous witness for all time. The example of their courage and steadfastness help us to know the way.

Jesus has prepared a place for us and will come again (John 14: 2-4).

Jesus reveals the essence of God's glorious plan of salvation and redemption of mankind: "I am going to prepare a place for you." That preparation involved Calvary, the Cross, and His ascension into Heaven. He gives us the promise that He will come back for His own and take us to be with Him. When those who belong to Christ close their eyes on this world, there is a place in Heaven for them to go, a place that was prepared for them by Jesus.

> Mark 13:26-27: "At that time, men will see the Son of Man coming in clouds with great power and glory. And he will send his angels and gather his elect from the four winds, from the ends of the earth to the ends of the heavens."

2. **Jesus is the only way to God and is Truth and Life (John 14:5-6).**

   JESUS IS THE WAY

   > John 14:3-4: "And if I go and prepare a place for you, I will come back and take you to be with me that you also may be where I am. You know the way to the place where I am going."

In John 14:5, Thomas asks the question that reveals what all the disciples were probably thinking: "We don't even have a clue about the way or the place where you say you are going."

One thing that you have to give Thomas credit for is that he takes his confusion and his questions directly to the source, and we can learn from his example. Thomas doesn't call up the other disciples and speculate about the "what and why" of what Jesus said; he directs his question to Jesus. Jesus, in turn, makes the assertion to the confused disciples that they do know the way to where He is going. The Savior patiently responds to Thomas, giving the disciples more revelations about His character and His relationship with the Father.

I encourage those seeking a relationship with Jesus, those already in a relationship, and those wanting to strengthen their relationship, to take their issues, fears, doubts, questions directly to Jesus with expectant hearts. Then, await your answer. If you struggle to understand a specific doctrine, principle, or Bible truth, grab hold to what you can understand and apply that to your life. Give the rest to God, and ask Him to open the eyes of your understanding and trust that He will help you get the rest of it. Don't let your confusion or lack of understanding be a stumbling block for you. For me, once I began studying the Bible in a more in-depth way, I discovered that there were many doctrines and truths I didn't know or understand. Many people in my study groups seemed to have substantially superior Bible knowledge than I, and that was intimidating. I often struggled with my Bible Study lessons and questions. Finally, I learned not to stress about what I didn't know or understand, and I didn't let it cause me to quit or give up. I found God to be true to His Word. Because I was seeking Him, He let me be found of Him, and I found understanding. Jesus doesn't want us to be confused about Him or the truths in His Word. We can humbly approach Him with our questions, confusion, and doubts. He will give us answers and open the eyes of our understanding. Now, let's get back to Thomas.

Thomas is confused about "The Way" and doesn't realize he is looking at and speaking to "The Way." Jesus goes on to give the disciples and believers a roadmap and tells them that the road to God runs straight through Him. There are no other routes, byways, or detours around him. Jesus opens the way for mankind to be reconciled back to God through His substitutionary death on the Cross that atoned for our sins. From His place on the throne in Heaven, seated at the right hand of the Father, Jesus continues to help us know the way as He acts as our Great High Priest Who intercedes and advocates for us.

Many non-Christians feel insulted by and flat out reject this foundational principle of Christian doctrine that Jesus is the only way to God. We are accused of being arrogant, non-inclusive, and intolerant by other religions whose belief systems may insist there are many paths to God, or that their path is the only way. I was taught to respect other peoples' beliefs and religions, even if they differ from my own, and that we are all created and loved by God. But I am going to have to stand on God's Word as truth.

JESUS IS TRUTH

"What is truth?"

Pilate poses this rhetorical question to Jesus in John 18:37-38. Jesus has been brought to Pilate by the Jewish Leaders who are demanding that Pilate crucify Jesus.

Pilate interrogates Jesus and seeks the answer to the burning question of that day. "Jesus: Who are you?" Jesus tells Pilate the reason He was born, and His purpose for coming into this world was to bear witness to the truth, and that everyone on the side of truth listens to Him. Pilate sensed the truth but was held captive to the drama of the situation and his own ambitions. In spite of his reservations and the warning from his wife, Pilate succumbed to the pressures of the Jewish leaders and the crowds and ordered Jesus crucified.

Pilate had the personification and the embodiment of truth standing right before him. Pilate rejected Jesus and the truth at the very moment Pilate needed it most because the truth is freeing; it has power, and it is a spiritual weapon of warfare (Ephesians 6:13-14). Like Pilate, for some people, truth is relevant to the situation at hand, the momentary need, or the moral standards of the day, but the pure truth that Jesus spoke about is constant. From the beginning of time until the end of the ages, it will not vary one iota. Like Pilate, the "world" rejects God, is indifferent to the truths of His Word, and is engaged in an ongoing battle to assert itself over God. Therefore, we must equip ourselves with the weapons of warfare that God has given us so that we can do combat with untruths like false doctrine, error, worldliness, and sinful behavior.

Believers are called to flip the script on the world by rejecting the world's lies and asserting God's Word in its place. With the John 14 Roadmap, Jesus tells us the route we are to take to accomplish this.

> Romans 1:25: They exchanged the truth about God for a lie and worshiped and served created things rather than the Creator—who is forever praised. Amen.

JESUS IS LIFE

> John 11:43-44: "...Jesus called in a loud voice, "Lazarus, come out!" The dead man came out, his hands and feet wrapped with strips of linen, and a cloth around his face. Jesus said to them, "Take off the grave clothes and let him go."

Jesus performed many astounding miracles, but raising Lazarus from the dead was over the top. It was an awe-inspiring demonstration of Jesus' power and divine authority over both life and death. Lazarus loved and was beloved of Jesus. He had fallen gravely ill in Bethany, and his desperate sisters sent for Jesus, hoping that Jesus would save him. Despite the sisters' urgency,

Jesus delayed going to Lazarus because He knew that Lazarus' death and dramatic resurrection was going to glorify God. I want to believe if I had been on the fence about believing in Jesus and had been present for or heard of Lazarus' resurrection, that would have sealed the deal for me.

By the time Jesus got to Lazarus, Lazarus had been dead for four days, and his sister Mary had an attitude about Jesus taking so long to come. When God doesn't respond to your prayers when and how you want Him to, how does that affect your feelings about Him? Jesus ministers to both of the grief-stricken sisters and reveals that He is the resurrection and life and that those who believe in Him will have eternal life. Lazarus heard Jesus' voice calling him to come out of the tomb; he obeyed Jesus' call and crossed over from death to life. Jesus is calling you to come to Him and to cross over from death to eternal life through His power, and because of His victory over death. He is also calling you to come to Him and come out from among this hurting, dying world. Do you hear his voice? Like Lazarus, are you obediently answering His call?

Then, there was the issue of the grave clothes; coming out of the tomb, Lazarus was bound up in grave clothes that constricted him. Having resurrected Lazarus back into life, Jesus didn't want him to be bound up in any old things that restricted or hindered him, and He doesn't want that for you either. You are beloved of Jesus, and He will empower you to break free from sin and sinful habits that have their binding grip on you.

What situations in your life seem dead and hopeless?

Is it your marriage, finances, weaknesses, or addictions?

Are your children's behaviors breaking your heart?

Know that Jesus is able to breathe life into your struggle and resurrect that which looks dead to your natural eye.

Also, in the resurrection of Lazarus, we see that Jesus is the source of life and has supreme God-given authority over both life and death. Jesus, the life-giver, gives us: physical life, spiritual life, eternal life, a new life, a delivered life, and a life of freedom. Jesus said, "I am the bread of life. Whosoever comes to me will never go hungry, and whosoever believes in me will never be thirsty" (John 6:35). He is the source of our spiritual nourishment and the sustenance that will fill, strengthen, and sustain us.

3. Jesus and God are One (John 14:7-11).

> John 14:7-8: *If you really know me, you will know my Father as well. From now on, you do know him and have seen him."* Philip said, *"Lord, show us the Father, and that will be enough for us."*

Jesus has told the disciples about his deity and that He and God are one. The dazed, confused disciples don't get this concept either. Philip, one of the first disciples Jesus called, is asking the question that is probably in the hearts of all the other disciples. I can relate to Philip in this situation because some Christian doctrines such as Deity, The Godhead, The Trinity, and Eternal Security are not easy to understand. You may have been a Christian for a long time but still not have a full understanding. I have been one of those people that didn't know what I should have known. I was a Christian for many years before I got some real understanding regarding the role of the Holy Spirit. The Holy Spirit is a critical member of the Trinity, and I describe my journey of getting to know Him better in more detail later in Part 7 of this section.

Believers have a responsibility to study God's Word, grow, and mature in our Faith. We don't have to work for our salvation; however, we do have to work at our spiritual growth. Consider Nicodemus, a seeker of the truth about Jesus (John 3:1-15). Nicodemus was a Jew, a Pharisee, a

Teacher, and a member of the Sanhedrin (The Jewish Ruling Council). Highly credentialed, he was a "big shot" in the religious establishment that was at odds with Jesus. Jesus' teachings had evidently resonated with Nicodemus and perhaps had even convicted Nicodemus' heart. He didn't understand all of it, but it was apparent to Nicodemus that God was in the mix of what Christ was doing and saying. Needing more information, more understanding, he went directly to the source for answers, but he went to Jesus at night in the dark. With his self-worth and confidence based on his credentials and his Jewish heritage, Nicodemus wasn't ready to jeopardize his position of power yet by being seen with Jesus.

Yet, Jesus didn't cast Nicodemus out because Nicodemus came to Jesus secretively at night. Jesus met Nicodemus right where he was and began teaching him, telling him that the way to God was through "new" birth in Jesus by water and of the Holy Spirit. This is the Ministry of Regeneration and is the beginning of Jesus being born in us.

Here's how the Ministry of Regeneration works: as we die to our flesh and discontinue living by our old sinful nature, we are born anew in Jesus, and begin living by His Spirit. It's a process of being regenerated into newness of life in Christ by the power of the Holy Spirit. Nicodemus was a teacher and a prominent man in Jewish religious circles, but there were things he should have known that he didn't know, and Jesus pointed that out to him. I can relate to not knowing spiritual things I should have known, can you? Jesus doesn't cast us out when we come humbly before Him, seeking answers. He is our Teacher. Jesus doesn't want us to be in the dark about Him. If we seek Him, He will give us answers, and His truth will bring us out of the darkness into His marvelous light. By the way, this encounter ends, you could be left wondering what became of Nicodemus.

Did he accept Jesus and the great spiritual truths that Jesus tried to teach him that night? Yes, he became a believer. In John 7:50-51, we see Nicodemus taking a stand against the conspiratorial Jewish leaders as he urges them to give Jesus a fair hearing before judging Jesus.

After the crucifixion, Nicodemus works with Joseph of Arimathea to get Pilate's permission to obtain Jesus' body to be embalmed and placed in Joseph's tomb (John 19:8-40). Something happens when you meet Jesus, and when you come into the presence of Jesus. Things happen. Things change. You change. In John 14:7-11, Jesus the Son continues giving out revelations and truths about Himself and His deep union with God the Father. He tells us that He was not out there going rogue, randomly talking off the top of His head, acting on His own, but that God authorized the words He spoke and the work He did.

How do you ever really know who a person is? You can know someone for a very long time, think you know him or her well, then the person acts in a way that makes you discover things that you never suspected. Jesus wants us to connect with Him and His Father on a deep, personal level, and know with certainty that one day Jesus and God won't suddenly change up on us as people often do. Jesus can help us understand God because Jesus is the perfect revelation and reflection of God. Moreover, Jesus was the perfect manifestation of God's attributes and God's will. God lived through Him, spoke through Him, and worked through Him. Our relationship with Jesus and God mirrors that deep union because They live in us and work through us.

God's Final Word: His Son

> Hebrews 1:1-3: *In the past, God spoke to our ancestors through the prophets at many times and in various ways, but in these last days he has spoken to us by his Son, whom he appointed heir of all things, and through whom also he made the universe. The Son is the radiance of God's glory and the exact representation of his being, sustaining all things by his powerful word.*

Believe, Believe!!!

Jesus said, "I am in the Father, and the Father is in me," and then He gives the confused disciples two reasons why Philip and all his disciples should believe this.

(1) Because Jesus had told them.
(2) Because the works they had seen Jesus do were the evidence that bore witness to it.

Jesus understands that this is a confusing concept/truth for them to grasp. However, He assures them that when they meditate on His words and combine them with the miracles they have seen Him perform, it will lead to understanding and unshakable belief in Him.

4. Jesus' Followers Will Do Great Works (John 14:12).

If you belong to Jesus, then He promises that you will do great works. He teaches that those who believe in Him will do the works He did, or even greater. What does Jesus mean when He says that we would do greater works than He? Are believers going to be resurrecting people from the dead, walking on water, giving sight to the blind, and healing lepers? We are awed by the spectacular miracles and healings that Jesus performs. But those spectacular miracles always symbolized a deeper spiritual meaning: such as a spiritual cleansing, spiritual healing or spiritual rebirth. Jesus' greatest work was to lay down His life for us, thereby reconciling us back to God. We are called by Jesus to continue His work in the Ministry of Reconciliation by showing others the way to God. Our first and most important "work" is to believe.

We are to do works of love that point to Jesus and bear witness to others that we are indeed connected to Him and living a new life in Him. We are to tell others about Him and the message of the gospel. We are to bring others to Him. Do people who know and interact with you see the love of Jesus Christ reflected through you? The drawing power of Jesus' love is so strong that His love displayed in you is able to draw people to Him. Would a nonbeliever be able to look at your life and see a difference in you versus what they see in the world? Would they desire for themselves what they see in you and seek God because of it? Yes, God is still in the miracle business today, and resurrections and healings can and do occur. But the greater works, the the greatest work for us is to believe and lead others to Him.

Spiritual Gifts, Anointed Talents, and God-Given Skills

Jesus said that those who belong to Him would be empowered to do great works. In addition to bringing others to Jesus, we are to do works of service for the edification and growth of Jesus' kingdom. God gives us gifts and talents to be used to do His work, so we need to know what our

gifts are and use them for His purposes. We are given three lists of spiritual gifts and ministry gifts in Romans 12:6-8, 1 Corinthians 12: 4-11, and Ephesians 4:11-13. Spiritual gifts are given to every Christian by the Holy Spirit and by Christ himself. God also gives us talents, and He anoints some of those talents specifically for service to Him. We are called to use our spiritual gifts and God-given talents in humble service to God with diligence and joy.

Bezalel and Oholiab

Exodus 31:1-6: Then the Lord said to Moses, "See, I have chosen Bezalel son of Uri, the son of Hur, of the tribe of Judah, and I have filled him with the Spirit of God, with wisdom, with understanding, with knowledge and with all kinds of skills... 6 Moreover, I have appointed Oholiab son of Ahisamak, of the tribe of Dan, to help him. Also, I have given ability to all the skilled workers to make everything I have commanded you."

Just as God equipped these craftsmen in Exodus 31:1-6 with skills to build his Tabernacle, Jesus will equip you to do the works needed to build His body, the Church. He calls us to continue His work by using our spiritual gifts and talents to help Jesus' church grow and become stronger. As we minister to and serve others, we are glorifying His name and helping to show the way to Christ. You may not be healing people and raising them from the dead, but there are important works that Jesus is calling you to do. He has given you gifts and talents and will anoint them for His purposes. Don't be confused about them, and don't let them go to waste. The Holy Spirit also helps show us the way by giving us spiritual gifts and by guiding us in their use. Use your gifts to help others to know the way to Him.

5. Jesus' Name Has Power (John 14:13-14).

Yes, There Is Something About That Name!

Many gospel songs tell us that "there is something about the name of Jesus." What is it about that name? A review of the Scriptures tells us a great deal about the power, the blessings, and the miracles that flow from the name of Jesus.

In Philippians 2:9, we are told that Jesus was exalted by God and given a name above every name.

> *Philippians 2:9-11: Therefore God exalted him to the highest place and gave him the name that is above every name, that at the name of Jesus every knee should bow, in heaven and on earth and under the earth, and every tongue acknowledge that Jesus Christ is Lord, to the glory of God, the Father.*

God exalted Jesus to the highest place of honor and gave Him a name above all others. We are to follow God's example by honoring and revering that name. It is a name that saves, a name in which we are to place our faith, belief, and trust. One day, every knee will bow down in worship to that name, and every tongue will utter a confession of His exalted Lordship.

Miracles Happen: Power Flows When We Call on the Name of Jesus

As the Apostles went about their work of evangelizing the world after Jesus' resurrection, they remembered what Jesus had told them about asking in His name. They came to rely on that name, and in the New Testament, we see examples of the Apostles using it freely, frequently, and boldly. We see action and activity initiated by the Apostles in the name of Jesus in conjunction with the power of the Holy Spirit. Here are some examples, along with their scriptural references:

> *Repentance, Baptism, and Forgiveness of Sins (Acts 2:38)*
>
> *Washing, Sanctification, and Justification (1 Cor. 6:11)*
>
> *Miraculous Healings (Acts 3:5-7, 16)*
>
> *Deliverances (Acts 16:17-19)*
>
> *Fearless Preaching (Acts 9:27-28)*
>
> *Appeal for Unity (1 Cor 1:10)*
>
> *Judgment (1 Cor. 5:3)*

> Thanksgiving (Ephesians 5:20)
> Prayers for the Sick (James 5:14)

Today, believers still have access to "that name" and the power behind it. We should learn to use it as boldly as the Apostles did. But we need to do it correctly.

You May Ask Me for Anything in My Name, and I Will Do It.

At the time that I wrote this book, my car was eleven years old; I was very attached to her. I tend to keep my cars until they can't go any longer, and after having them for ten to twelve years, they become like children to me. People could say I am the quintessential "little old lady driver," so my cars tend to have very low mileage and remain in very good condition. When I bought the car, its technology was state of the art, but car technology changed a lot during the eleven years I owned it. I am a lightweight techie, and after I saw the evolution of navigation systems, USB ports, and iPad connectivity, I wanted all of those things. Should I have just prayed in the name of Jesus and asked for a new car? Didn't God say He would give us the desires of our heart? Is this what Jesus is talking about when He says that if I ask anything in His name, He will give it to me? Didn't He say in Matthew

7:7 that I was to ask, seek, and knock on the door? Can't I just name it and claim it?

In John 14: 13-14, Jesus is speaking not so much about self-centered prayers about our wants and desires but about requests that will generate fruit for the Kingdom and bring glory to God. That's how we see the disciples praying in Jesus' name in the New Testament Scriptures cited in the previous section. The disciples also are praying for things that are in line with the will and the character of Jesus. To use someone's name to request things that contradict the essence and nature of that person is perpetrating fraud, and it definitely won't work. Many Scriptures in the Old Testament encourage us to take our petitions and desires to God and promises us that He will meet our needs even unto abundance. Jesus had spoken about and taught parables about how God answers our prayers. But in John 14:13-14, Jesus does a new thing. He reveals that there is power in His name and gives us the privilege of using His name as a point of access to His power. The precious and exalted name of Jesus has miraculous power flowing from it. Savior is the meaning of His name, and rightfully so since He is the Captain of our salvation. The apostles were the first ones to call on and rely on his name. Follow their example.

6. **Jesus Says That Loving Him Means Obeying Him (John 14:15, 21, 23-24).**

In John 14:15, 21, 23-24, Jesus gives us a big clue as to who belongs to him and who loves Him. Those who belong to Him are those who obey Him. In essence, He is saying that obedience to His will, His words, and His ways is one of the important proofs of our love for Him. If you are married or in a romantic relationship, there are "acts of love" that you will demonstrate on a continual basis to keep that relationship alive and healthy. You might send flowers, love notes, cards, buy gifts, etc. The method or way you express your love depends on your "love language."

We are encouraged to try to learn our partners' love language and deal with our partners in a way that speaks to his or her preferred love language. The love language Jesus is requesting of us is obedience, which is one very important way He says we demonstrate our love for Him.

When you were growing up, there were certain things that your parents repeated to you because they were important, and your parents wanted to make sure you understood it. Some examples might be: don't open the door to strangers; be very careful who you hang around; always wear a seatbelt, etc. In that same mindset of "repeat it because it's vital," Jesus restates His "love and obedience" requirement in verse 21 and then again in verse 23. Just in case we still don't get the importance of this point, in verse 24, He gives it to us in reverse, saying that "anyone who does not love me does not obey my teachings." Jesus, our example in all things, goes one step further in vs. 31.

As He lifts up His obedience to His Father as an example for us to follow, He states, "...I love the father and do exactly what my father has commanded me."

Jesus was obedient to His father, even unto the Cross and the grave. Obedience is a key theme throughout the Bible. There are sixty-six books of the Bible, and obedience is mentioned in thirty-six of them, 242 times. We often pray asking God to do what we want Him to do or what we feel we need Him to do for us. But are you doing what He has asked you to do? Jesus wants us to walk the walk and talk the talk. Our obedience to God is the actions on our part that witness to the world as to whom we love. Our disobedience to God also witnesses to the world about our love for God and the state of our relationship with Him.

Knowing we will never be able to walk in obedience in our own strength with our weak flesh, Jesus promises to send us a helper. This helper will show us the way and help us to become more and more like Christ. Obey God not just because it's our calling, but because it pleases God.

> 1 John 5:3: "For this is the love of God, that we keep his commandments."

Jesus tells us that you can't really love Him in the way He desires you to love Him if you don't obey Him. The two go hand in hand. He wants the unbelieving world to see your example of obedience to help show them the way to Him.

7. **Jesus Gives Us the Promise of The Holy Spirit Who Will Help Show Us The Way (John 14:16-20, 25-26).**

John 14:16 – 17: And I will ask the Father, and He will give you another advocate to help you and be with you forever— the Spirit of truth. The world cannot accept Him, because it neither sees Him nor knows Him. But you know Him, for He lives with you and will be in you.

My Journey with Understanding and Getting to Know the Holy Spirit

To say that The Holy Spirit is a big subject is an understatement. It is a subject big enough to fill its own book, and a massive book at that. I will attempt to do a brief overview of the Holy Spirit, primarily focusing on what Jesus teaches us about Him in the discourse of John 14-17. For many years, The Holy Spirit was the part of the Trinity I was least familiar with and left me the most confused. I was raised Episcopalian, a denomination that has a very reverential, ceremonial, and quiet style of worship. Charismatics would describe it as "dry." I attended Immaculate Conception Catholic School from grades eight through ten, which included attending Mass every Friday. I thought that the Catholic Mass was a beautiful worship service which was very similar in style to the Episcopalian service. However, the manner in which those two denominations worshipped when I was growing up was very, very different from the Black Baptist or A.M.E. (African Methodist Episcopal) type of worship experience. Also, the music was very different, and I grew up as a Southern black girl raised in the Church who knew a lot of hymns but didn't know a lot of gospel music. I'll never forget the first time I attended a Holiness worship service. People were speaking in tongues, dancing, running, and falling out.

Me with my Episcopalian, Catholic School, reserved self, I didn't know quite what to make of it all. I knew what I was seeing was Holy, but I didn't fully understand it. I remember thinking, "I'm not sure what all of this is, and I'm certainly not feeling what these people are feeling. "Should I be?"

And if I'm not, is there something wrong with me; do I know and love God as much as these people do? Throughout my Christian life, there have been times that I have been made to feel like the odd man out because I didn't worship with more emotion. On the other end of the spectrum, I am aware of people who get annoyed and even demean a spirit-filled, charismatic worship experience because, to them, "it doesn't take all of that."

Speaking in tongues is not a gift that has been given to me yet. Although I've wanted to do so, it hasn't happened. I think I've gotten close, but it still didn't happen. It's even crossed my mind to force it or just do it of self because I have heard ministers say every Christian should speak in tongues. I've been knocked in the head in Worship services and should have fallen out "slain in the Spirit," but it didn't happen to me when others around me were falling out right and left. It made me think something was lacking in me. For a long time, I thought being filled with the Holy Spirit simply meant speaking in tongues, falling out, dancing, shouting, and running in a church service, as I had seen in charismatic churches. I thought the main purpose of the Holy Spirit was to show up and make Himself evident in worship service. As I grew spiritually, I realized that I had such an erroneous, extremely narrow view of the role of the Holy Spirit as defined by what I had seen in those charismatic church services. After studying scriptures and teaching about the Holy Spirit, I was shocked to discover how limited my understanding was about this important member of the Trinity. I came to realize this is what happens when we come to conclusions based solely on what we think or what we feel and not God's Word. We end up in a place of error, confusion, or limited understanding.

Even though I have yet to speak in tongues or fallen out slain in the spirit, I have come to understand that the Holy Spirit has most definitely manifested Himself in me through the writing of this book. Without His leading, there is no way in the world this book could have come forth from me. Jesus certainly doesn't want us to be confused about the Holy Spirit, who is such an important member of the Trinity. Jesus is the one who gave us some of our first teaching about the Holy Spirit, much of it in the John 14-17 discourse.

THE HOLY SPIRIT AT CREATION

The Holy Spirit was present at creation and involved in the creation of the world and man. Also, He was powerfully present and active throughout the Old Testament with many references to His "coming upon" the people of the Old Testament and making things happen. He was active in the earthly ministry of Jesus Christ as recorded in the Gospels. On the day of Pentecost, The Holy Spirit made a dramatic, fiery, grand entrance into his new role of indwelling believers of Jesus Christ (Acts 1). The Book of Acts is known as the "Acts of the Apostles." Still, it could also rightfully be known as the Acts of the Holy Spirit since the Holy Spirit is all over the book of Acts, working in the Apostles and through circumstances to ensure the establishment of Jesus' Church in the earth realm. And throughout the New Testament, in the physical absence of Jesus, we have the physical indwelling presence of the Holy Spirit guiding, protecting, and enabling God's people to accomplish the "Great Commission" that was given to them by Christ.

Just as God and Jesus were active and present at the beginning of creation, so was the Holy Spirit. The Holy Spirit was so present in the beginning that He is mentioned in the second sentence of the first chapter of the first book of the Bible:

> *Genesis 1:1-2: In the beginning, God created the heavens and the earth. Now the earth was formless and empty, darkness was over the surface of the deep, and the Spirit of God was hovering over the waters.*

A few verses later in Genesis 1:26, as God prepares to make man, God uses the plural words "us" and "our," saying, "Let us make mankind in our image, in our likeness..." Bible Scholars interpret the words "us" and "our" as references in that verse as meaning the Trinity: God, Jesus, and the Holy Spirit. The creative powers of the Holy Spirit were involved in creating the world and creating man. And just as the Holy Spirit was involved in creating this world and creating you, that creative power can flow into whatever problems, situations, ministry, or needs you have resulting in those things being creatively worked out to the Glory of God.

The Holy Spirit and the People of the Old Testament

There are many references to the Holy Spirit throughout the Old Testament. In this context, He is usually referred to as the Spirit of The Lord. Before the day of Pentecost, the Holy Spirit did not indwell men. He came upon them, worked in them, or through them. Scriptures refer to the Holy

Spirit's coming upon many of the great Saints of the Old Testament, such as Moses, Gideon, Samson, Saul, David, Elijah, and Ezekiel, naming a few. And when the Holy Spirit came upon the scene, He brought the power, might, and miraculous action with him. Throughout the Old Testament, He stirred people into action, empowered leaders, led God's people in warfare, spoke through the prophets, equipped people to do God's work, gave instructions, and gave warnings, among other things. There are instances in the Old Testament of the Holy Spirit's operating so powerfully in God's people that even the people of the world recognized that what was happening could only be because of the presence of the Spirit of God. In Gen 41:38, after hearing Joseph's God-given plan to handle the coming famine in Egypt, Pharaoh declared:

"Can we find anyone like this man, one in whom is the spirit of God?"

Would anyone make a statement like that about you and your life? Who is looking at you and can conclude that the Holy Spirit dwells within you? The Holy Spirit, as a member of the Trinity, has always been operating to help God's people to know the way and to do the work and the will of God. In John 14, Jesus is giving Him as a gift to believers in a new and special way. The Holy Spirit will now live in believers, thus connecting believers to Jesus and God forever.

The Holy Spirit and The Earthly Ministry of Jesus Christ

In Acts 10:38, we are told how "God anointed Jesus of Nazareth with the Holy Spirit and power." In Isaiah 11:2, the great Old Testament Prophet, Isaiah, foretold that the Spirit of the Lord would rest upon Jesus. When Jesus was in the Synagogue in Nazareth, someone handed Him the scroll from the Prophet Isaiah, and Jesus read aloud this prophecy about Himself, which speaks to the active role of the Holy Spirit in his ministry.

> Luke 4:18 – 19: *"The Spirit of the Lord is on me, because he has anointed me to proclaim good news to the poor. He has sent me to proclaim freedom for the prisoners and recovery of sight for the blind, to set the oppressed free, to proclaim the year of the Lord's favor."*

Jesus then told his audience that it was seeing and hearing the fulfillment of Isaiah's prophecy in Him. In each of the following major life events in the earthly ministry of Jesus, the Scriptures tell us that the Holy Spirit was there in the mix, creating, empowering, and even leading the action:

> The conception of Jesus (Matthew 1:17-19)
>
> The baptism of Jesus by John the Baptist (Matthew 3:16)
>
> The leading of Jesus into the desert for the Temptation (Matthew 4:1)
>
> The return of Jesus from the desert in the power of the Spirit (Luke 4:14)
>
> The resurrection of Jesus (Romans 8:11)

Just as The Holy Spirit was present and active in the big, the small, and for all of Jesus' life, so will He be for your life and all those who belong to Jesus.

What Jesus Teaches Us About the Ministry of The Holy Spirit

As Jesus prepares for His crucifixion, death, resurrection, and ascension, He promises His disciples that He won't leave them all alone as orphans, and He was going to ask God to send another advocate in His name to help them, and that this advocate would mark and seal believers as belonging to Him forever. Jesus' request was for **another** advocate for His disciples, **another**, as in of the same kind as Jesus Himself by literally taking Jesus' place, living within us, binding us in union with Jesus and God. How does the Holy Spirit advocate for us? He's our comforter, counselor, helper, encourager, guide, teacher, the revealer of truths and reminder of what Jesus taught.

The Holy Spirit is unseen, unknown, and unaccepted by a skeptical, unbelieving world. But He is seen, known, accepted, and living inside of those who belong to Christ. In John 16, Jesus goes on to teach us more about the ministry work of the Holy Spirit as His work relates to both believers and the unbelieving world. That work involves testifying about Jesus. It also involves convicting the world of sin, opening our eyes to Jesus's righteousness, and telling the world about how Jesus' judgment and victory over Satan has left Satan a condemned, defeated foe. And there's more help for those who belong to Jesus. The Holy Spirit helps to open the eyes of our understanding of all truths about Jesus. He receives, speaks, and reveals to us what Jesus wants to make known, including future events.

> 1 Corinthians 2:10:" ...these are the things God has revealed to us by his Spirit. The Spirit searches all things, even the deep things of God."

I want to share a situation in my life in which I clearly heard the voice of the Holy Spirit, but at the time, I didn't understand that it was Him speaking. I was hanging out with a childhood friend who had gotten deeply involved with drugs. He tried to get me to snort cocaine and was pressuring me to give it a try. Although at the time I was very young, in my early 20's, I was someone then who, for the most part, would go with the flow of things and was willing to experiment a bit. But I sensed that this was a line I shouldn't cross, and that snorting cocaine would have been a very wrong turn for my life. As my friend was pressing me to try it and was actually trying to put the cocaine to my nose, I clearly heard a voice say, "DON'T DO IT." The voice startled me and left me with a heightened sense that I was in some sort of danger. I then yelled out, "NO, I'M NOT DOING IT" and stood firmly, resisting my friend's continued pressure until he gave up. At that moment in my life, I was facing a choice that could have opened up my life to destruction. In this life, we have options, and sometimes we do make wrong choices.

Some of the consequences of bad choices can be overcome, but some consequences can be devastating and life-altering. When we walk with Jesus or when we are covered in prayer by others who do (parents, grandparents, family, friends), Jesus stands right there in the gap with us, protecting us in situations from others and even from ourselves.

On that night many years ago, The Holy Spirit spoke clearly and loudly to protect me from making a very disastrous choice for my life and guided me away from danger. Throughout my life, I have experienced the Holy Spirit doing all the things for me that Jesus promised He would, helping me to know the way. The Holy Spirit is a crucial person of the Trinity. Jesus gave the promise, the gift of the Holy Spirit, to his own to indwell them. The Holy Spirit has many critical roles in the life of a believer, helping to ensure we can always see and find the way.

8. Jesus Has Given Us His Peace (John 14:27).

The Peace of Jesus Christ

> John 14:27: "Peace I leave with you; my peace I give you. I do not give to you as the world gives. Do not let your hearts be troubled and do not be afraid."
>
> 2 Thessalonians 3:16: "Now may the Lord of peace himself give you peace at all times and in every way..."

Jesus, The Prince of Peace, The Lord of Peace, The Peace Giver, modeled peace during His life on earth and bequeathed it as a precious gift to His followers. How did He model peace? Throughout most of His ministry, the religious leadership in Israel was outraged that Jesus was challenging their status quo. They followed Him around, challenged, questioned, disputed, rejected, and conspired against Him. In response, He gave them His teachings, spoke hard truths to them, and chastised them. But Jesus always kept going, not letting anything or anyone distract Him from the work God had sent Him to do. The religious leadership's resistance was quite vigorous, but in handling their opposition, Jesus, our example in all things, showed us how to face down challenges and stay on point. For example, there were times during His ministry when there were crowd control issues, and the crowds almost got out of hand. There were also times when things were on the verge of getting physical (the crowd threatened to stone Him, John 8:59), and when things actually did become violent (i.e., His arrest, Peter's cutting off Malcheus' ear, John 18:10). And what about the days before His crucifixion? He was betrayed by a man who had been in His presence and sat under His teachings for over three years. He was abandoned and denied by His other disciples. He was dragged through a bunch of sham trials, mocked, spat upon, beaten. He was hauled before Herod, the "beheader" of John the Baptist, and hauled before Pilate, a leader who didn't have the courage or fortitude to do what he knew to be right. He was brutalized, paraded through the streets of Jerusalem in a weakened state, carrying a heavy cross that bore our sin and shame. He was nailed to and hung on that cross. He then battled death, Satan, and the grave to claim the Victory for us.

Jesus did not have a trouble-free time on this earth. But He was able to operate in peace and with an inner calm when things were getting really crazy in His circumstances. He told us that in this life we are going to have troubles, but with His peace fortifying us, we will "go through" and

"get through" those troubles, because He has overcome the world for us. He has given us his peace, not just any peace, but a peace that comes from Him. His peace empowers us to go through the turbulent circumstances that come into our lives with calmness and strength that are of Him, and without which, we would surely succumb to fear, confusion, and error. He is the "rebuker" of storms and the calmer of storms. He is in the boat with us, His care of us never falters, and He most certainly doesn't want us to drown (Mark 8:35-41).

Jesus is our example in all things, and He gave us His example of how to operate in peace while under the most conflict-laden, challenging, and brutal circumstances. He also gave us that peace that comes from and is of Him. Operating in His peace is the only way we would ever be able to face some of life's hard challenges and stay sane.

Jesus' Peace Versus the World's Version of Peace

Jesus paid the high price for our salvation and our peace with God through His sacrifice and death on the cross. Isaiah 53:5 tells us that Jesus suffered greatly (was pierced, crushed) and that the chastisement of our peace was upon Him so that He could bridge our separation from God brought about by sin. He is our peace, and His gospel of the good news is a gospel of peace. During His ministry, He often spoke and taught about peace. He sent people away after healing them and removing the thing that was disturbing their peace, telling them to go in peace.

Jesus' peace is a very different version from the world's version of peace. Several well-known Christmas Carols and hymns speak of Peace on Earth and Goodwill toward men. We sing our hearts out about it and long for it, but peace on this earth has always been elusive. As I wrote this book, our country had been engaged in war in Iraq and Afghanistan for over fifteen years. There are continuing outbreaks of battles between Israel and Palestine. Hotspots of rebellion, terrorism, conflict, and tension have forever manifested themselves all over this earth. Man can't even maintain peace within the bounds of his own family unit, let alone the whole world. History has proven that man is incapable of finding and sustaining peace. Jesus Christ is the only one who will be able to establish any lasting peace in your heart, in your family, or on earth.

Peace Stealers and How to Do Battle Against Them

Jesus blessed us so richly by giving us His peace. His peace is more wonderful than the world can even understand. It's like a protective covering over our hearts that guards against the peace stealers that come against us. Our part is to grab hold to His peace and hold on for dear life because this life is full of peace stealers. Peace-stealers are the people, situations and circumstances that come like thieves into our lives to bring confusion, challenges, and fear. God tells us to seek Him first and then to let Him add the "everything else." Peace and love are His will for our lives. In today's world, people concentrate on getting the "everything else." Many people are seeking everything but God. If he is even a factor in their strivings, he is a mere afterthought. Thus, as we strive for "stuff" instead of God, we can find ourselves outside of

God's will, which is an unsafe place to live and a place where your sense of peace will always be unsettled.

The Battle Plan for Handling Peace Stealers (Straight from The Bible)

The best way to start to combat anything is with prayer and the power of God's Word. As you are developing your battle plan, an excellent place to start is with the Bible. It doesn't matter what the issue is; God has a word for it. The Bible has much to say about peace:

> *If confusion is prevailing in a situation, then God is not in it (1 Cor 14:33).*
>
> *A disruption of your peace is an indicator that something is off. You should follow your peace (Heb. 12:14).*
>
> *Let peace rule your heart, not fear and confusion (Col. 3:15).*
>
> *Sometimes, you need to be physically still (Mark 4:39).*

There is a correlation between righteousness and peace. Peace is a fruit of righteousness and fruit of the Holy Spirit. If peace is present, righteousness is there.

> *Conversely, if confusion is present, wickedness and sin are somewhere in the mix (Gal 5:22).*
>
> *Jesus invites you into a place of peace. He invites you to come unto Him, learn from Him, take His yoke upon you, and receive rest (Mat 11:28-30).*
>
> *Set your mind on the Spirit and the things of God and keep it there (Rom. 8:6).*
>
> *Perfect peace is available to you if you keep your mind stayed on God and trust Him (Is. 26:3).*
>
> *Great peace is available to you if you love and obey God's word (Is. 54:10).*
>
> *Pursue Peace. As far as you are able, try to live in peace. Resist getting even, let God handle that part (Rom. 14:17-19, Rom. 12:17).*
>
> *There is a good future for the man of peace (Ps. 37:37).*

9. JESUS GAVE US THE JOHN 14 ROADMAP

At the beginning of Part 1 of this book, I spoke about the Romans Roadmap, which is a widely used Christian evangelizing tool. The final destination on the Romans Roadmap is Jesus. Grab hold of Him, accept him as your Savior, and never let go of Him. The title of Part I of this book is: JESUS LEAVES A ROADMAP IN THE GOSPEL OF JOHN POINTING THE WAY.

I spoke about seeing a second Roadmap that Jesus outlined in John 14 that will help His followers know the way to grow and mature in our walk with Him. Let's take a stroll down the John 14 Roadmap as Jesus shows us how to navigate our journey with Him victoriously.

The journey starts with faith, belief, and trust in Jesus and God.

Things from the John 14 Roadmap that Jesus wants you to know about Him:

> *He and His Father Can Be Trusted to Cover, Keep and Protect You.*
>
> *He has prepared a place for you (believers) and will come again.*
>
> *He is The Way to God.*
>
> *He is Truth and Life.*
>
> *He and God are One.*

Things on the John 14 Roadmap that Jesus has given us to facilitate our Growth and Sanctification:

- The Promise and Challenge of Doing Great Works
- Spiritual Gifts, Anointed Talents, and God-Given Skills

- Access to The Power in His Name
- The Promise That What We Ask for In His Name He Will Do
- The Demand to Show Our Love for Him By Obeying Him
- The Promise of the Holy Spirit Who Will Indwell / Live in Us
- His Peace

Part 2:

JESUS INVITES YOU TO ABIDE IN HIM AND LET HIS SPIRIT DWELL IN YOU TO SHOW YOU THE WAY (JOHN 15)

John's gospel is one of my favorite books in the Bible. Jesus' discourses in John 14, 15, 16, and 17 are absolutely beautiful, and I have a special love for Jesus' words in those chapters. For me, John 15 was a difficult chapter. Jesus is talking about things like vines, branches, pruning, fruit, lack of fruit, love, obedience, hatred, rejection, and persecution. The difficulty for me was what to make of all that. It is a very rich, meaty chapter, loaded with metaphors, allegories and symbolism. It's the kind of chapter you need to hang out in and meditate on to get to the depth of what Jesus is trying to tell us.

Do you know what your position is in Christ? In John 15, Jesus paints a picture of our position in Him and His expectations of us. He describes what a relationship with Him should be about -connection, union. I love how Christians have recently begun embracing the term relationship, using it instead of the term religious to define ourselves. Jesus tells us He wants to be in a connected relationship with us and describes it as an intimate union through which we receive the spiritual nourishment, which we need to be transformed and fruitful for His purposes. He also describes not being properly connected to Him and being apart from Him. He tells us that in that unconnected state, we in and of ourselves can do nothing. You shouldn't be apart from the One for Whom you were set apart. Know and stay in your position.

Jesus uses an interesting term to describe the connection He desires with us - ABIDING.

Definitions and synonyms of ABIDING are:

- to stay or live somewhere
- to remain or continue
- to endure without yielding, withstand
- to accept without objection
- to remain stable or fixed in a state

ABIDE IN JESUS THE TRUE VINE
(John 15:1)

"Stay joined to me," "dwell in," and "take care to live in me" are some of the terms used for abiding in different versions of the Bible in John 15. These terms could be characterized as "feel-good sayings," but exactly how do you apply them to your life? If Jesus tells us He desires something of us, we can trust that He will show us the way to make it happen. Let's look at how He describes in detail what abiding in Him looks like in John 15.

In John 15:1, Jesus declares that "I am the true vine, and my Father is the gardener." What an interesting choice of symbols. Of all the symbols Jesus could have used to describe His desired relationship with His own why did He choose a vine? A grapevine parallels the believer's relationship with the Lord in many ways. Grapevines are plants that require close care if they are to become productive. Their vines can produce fruit over a very long period of time — up to 100 years —, and they can be prolific producers, with one vine producing as much as 80 pounds of grapes in a season. Also, for a vine to be a good and prolific producer, it must have a solid connection to a good root system whose growth must be trained and focused. Most importantly, the quality of the root system dictates the quality of the fruit, the branches, and the vine.

THE VINE AND THE NATION OF ISRAEL

There are numerous references in the Old Testament, which describe Israel as God's chosen vine planted by Him in His vineyard. The vine was an important and sacred symbol of ancient Israel. Also, at one time, it was on Israel's coins, and its image was placed over the main doors of Israel's synagogues. Jesus was the fulfillment of all that the sacred vine and vineyard represented to Israel. Israel was God's original vine, but Jesus was the True Vine, and He emphatically declared it.

In John 13 –14, Jesus and the disciples have been in the Upper Room, and then in vs. 14:31, Jesus says, "Come now; let us leave." Bible Scholars have concluded that they leave the Upper Room, and in John 15, they are headed to the Garden of Gethsemane. The route they would have taken would have been down into the Kidron Valley and up the slope of the Mount of Olives to the Garden of Gethsemane.

As they walk along this path, scholars conclude that they pass by the numerous vineyards surrounding Jerusalem. These vines would have been fresh with the marks of having been recently pruned. It was so like Jesus to use that which was familiar, relatable, and vital to His audience as teaching points. Jesus will do that for you, also. Come along. Let's join Jesus on this walk with His disciples, listen to His marvelous words, meditate on them, and ask Him to show us the way to apply them in our lives.

1. Abide in And Remain Connected to The Vine to Find Your Purpose And Be Fruitful (John 15: 2 - 4)

I have visited the Wine Country in California; when there were no grapes on the vines, I thought that the vines themselves were beautiful greenery. Although the vintners can appreciate the beauty of the grapeless vines, they fully expect and need those vines to produce grapes for them.

One thing that stands out in my memory about the vineyards I saw in California's Wine Country is how healthy the vines were. I don't remember seeing anything dead on them, which means that the vintners were hyper-attentive to them and vigilant about removing anything dead or diseased.

That's what Jesus said his Father does. Cuts off the non-fruit-bearing branches. Those who profess to be in Christ but don't honestly believe. Sometimes, there are people in the Church, the body of Christ, who are not productive or are counterproductive to the point of being stumbling blocks to the fruitful members and those young in their faith. Diseased branches can infect other branches, infect other vines, and potentially the whole vineyard. Sin is like a disease that can contaminate the branches with the potential to spread and affect the whole vineyard and must be pruned off.

God disciplines the true branches that are already producing good fruit for the Kingdom as He cuts them back. He removes things, people, and behaviors from us. God's pruning of us doesn't always feel good. In fact, it can be downright painful. The result of His pruning makes us branches stronger, thus, causing us to be fruitful and even more fruitful. My mother loved to garden and had three Crepe Myrtle trees in her front yard. They grew to be big, showy trees that I looked forward to enjoying in the summers. After she cut them back in late fall and their leaves fell off, I would look at those bare ugly stumps in the winter and marvel that such big, gorgeous trees and flowers could have come from those stumps.

Pruning is part of the "training" process vintners use to focus the direction of the growth of the branches. Branches that grow wild and undirected are, in essence, siphoning off the nutrition and energy of the other vines. Those vines may produce grapes, but they will produce even more grapes after they are pruned and trained.

God has a plan for our lives that includes work that he has called each of us to do. However, we shouldn't be out there doing it on our own, "growing wild" and untrained outside of God's direction and priorities when we are doing His work.

2. **ABIDE WITH CHRIST ON THE VINE AND REFLECT HIS CHARACTER TO THE WORLD (John 15:5-6,8)**

A grapevine does not produce branches of apples, and a tomato vine does not produce branches of kiwis. Jesus expects His branches to produce fruit that looks like Him, represents Him and draws others to Him. We have to stay connected to Him since He and His indwelling Spirit do the transformative work in us that results in us looking like him and generates drawing power to Him. We are unable to do it of self, and if you think you can do it apart from Him, let's just take a look at some of the people in our lives and how we handle them versus the way Jesus would have us handle them.

Who is the person in your life who really knows how to push your buttons? You thought you were finished with telling people off, losing it, "cussing" people out. But then "that" person shows up on the scene of your life with manipulations and messiness, taking you places you thought you had left in your past. You've been hurt, betrayed, lied on. You know who did it, and it was someone close, most likely family or someone you thought was a friend. You have tried to forgive and forget, but you keep thinking about it and continue getting angry, unable to believe "they" would do "that" to you. How about the person who is mean, jealous, narcissistic, or has any of a wide range of dysfunctional behaviors that make him or her almost impossible to deal with let alone love? Then there's the person for whom you would move to the other side of the world so that you wouldn't have to see or deal with him or her, but you can't move because they are your spouse, child, family member, boss or coworker in the next cubicle. I call them the people that keep us on our knees.

We know what our natural inclinations are in handling these challenging people. But Jesus calls us to reflect his Christlike character to them, as they are the very ones who most need to see Him in us. So, we say to Jesus, "Yes, I understand what you want of me, but how do you expect me to show this person ...love, joy, peace, forbearance, kindness, goodness, faithfulness, gentleness and self-control?* When the truth is, you really want to punch that person out and feel that it would be so satisfying to your flesh, not to mention it's what you think he or she needs and deserves. "They" are one of the reasons why we have to stay up on the vine, in our position in Christ, letting Him transform us away from what the flesh wants, moving us toward doing things the way He wants us to. If we do as He says - abide in Him, abide in His love, abide in and obey His word, He will cause us to hang up those boxing gloves and put them up in the closet with the "cuss" them out, tell-them-off desires. He will also help us win the ongoing struggle to keep those boxing gloves and fleshy desires up in the closet or to get them back up on the shelf when our flesh has pulled them down from the shelf and put them in play.

> *Galatians 5:22-23: "But the fruit of the Spirit is love, joy, peace, forbearance, kindness, goodness, faithfulness, gentleness, and self-control. Against such things there is no law..."

The point Jesus makes in His use of the vine allegory is that He expects those who belong to Him to produce fruit. There is a process that God uses to bring forth that fruit from us, and there is a certain way that fruit is supposed to look. None of that can happen unless we stay connected to Jesus.

For a long time, when I read of Jesus' speaking about fruitfulness in John 15, I understood it to mean generating fruitful work for the upbuilding of His kingdom: ministry work, missionary work, serving, teaching. I eventually came to a complete understanding that it was also about producing the Fruits of the Holy Spirit in me.

Do you have questions about what the Fruits of the Holy Spirit look like? I did. The following three passages give a pretty clear picture of what they are, what they are not, and what the fruits of the flesh are. What they are, in essence, is a description of the character of Jesus Christ:

> Galatians 5:19-23: "The acts of the flesh are obvious: sexual immorality, impurity and debauchery; idolatry and witchcraft; hatred, discord, jealousy, fits of rage, selfish ambition, dissensions, factions and envy; drunkenness, orgies, and the like. I warn you, as I did before, that those who live like this will not inherit the kingdom of God. But the fruit of the Spirit is love, joy, peace, forbearance, kindness, goodness, faithfulness, gentleness, and self-control. Against such things there is no law..."
>
> Philippians 2: 1-5: Therefore if you have any encouragement from being united with Christ, if any comfort from his love, if any common sharing in the Spirit, if any tenderness and compassion, then make my joy complete by being like-minded, having the same love, being one in spirit and of

> one mind. Do nothing out of selfish ambition or vain conceit. Rather, in humility value others above yourselves, not looking to your own interests but each of you to the interests of the others. In your relationships with one another, have the same mindset as Christ Jesus.

For the vintners in California Wine Country, quantity and the maximum output of grape production drives everything. The more grapes produced, the more money in the vintners' pockets. With God, it's different. It's as much about the quality of the fruit as it is about quantity, with quality measured by the glory it brings to Him. When we exhibit the Christlike characteristics described in the above passages, we will be able to produce the fruit Jesus says He desires of us as we lead others to Him and do works for the building up of His Kingdom. And God will get the glory.

3. ABIDE IN HIS WORD AND PRAY (John 15:7, 16)

We all know what happens when a leaf falls from a branch or when a branch falls off a vine. It is deprived of the nourishment it needs to survive, so it dies. Storms can blow through a vineyard and can do much damage by severing or partially severing some branches from the vine. As a result, treatment and repair will be needed to keep those dangling branches connected and producing, but if a branches' connection to the vine is lost, there will be no fruit harvested from those branches. Many threats in this world have the potential to jeopardize our connection to Christ. Storms blow into our lives, damaging and wounding us.

Disappointed and wounded, some of Jesus' branches let go and end up on the backslidden and fallen-away path. When I was a child, my brothers and I used to sit on the front porch, where we ate watermelons and spat the seeds in our front yard. Lo and behold, a watermelon vine with one watermelon sprouted in our front yard. We were so excited. We watched and pampered that watermelon as if it was a baby. "Is it ripe enough yet" was the question we asked almost every day as we inspected it and thumped it. Then one day, the watermelon was gone because one of the neighborhood kids had taken it. We were totally bummed out and ready to do war over "the crime." It wasn't ripe enough to be sweet when it was heisted, so it was totally wasted— plucked from the vine before its time. That incident reminds me of what happens to the backslidden or fallen-away believer who was connected to the vine. He or she has received the word, but the thief comes and steals it from his or her heart.

Severances and storms are not the only "thieves," which "steal" us away from God. Sin also separates us from God. You may find yourself caught up in some type of sin, and the weight of its guilt keeps you from Him, from going to His house or being around His people. Or you may be the one who keeps going to church, looks so Christian to others all while secretly being caught up in something that could lead to your destruction. That sin struggle has kept you from abiding in Him, His Word, and His freedom.

The Good News is that the treatment, deliverance, and healing needed may be received through the vine, and so we really must cling to Jesus and not let go. Look at the world we live in today with manic-like levels of activity and information. Distractions are everywhere competing for our attention. I liken them to the weeds in a vineyard, stubbornly and persistently growing while stretching forth up onto the vine, trying to choke the life out of the connection and break the branches away from God. A severed vine results in fruitlessness, and there are consequences for fruitlessness. Those consequences can affect you, your children, and your future generations. Jesus warns us about storm damage, pitfalls, sins, weeds, and fruitlessness. He also gives us spiritual tools to combat them.

In John 15:7, He speaks of two very powerful tools which are part of the believer's arsenal of weapons for warfare—the Word and Prayer (Eph. 6:10-18). In John 15, Jesus says that a very critical part of abiding is to have His words abide in us because, among other things, it has cleansing power. You have to open up the Bible and read it and do so on an ongoing basis to the extent that it becomes an enduring habit, a lifestyle.

Also, the Word of God helps us to identify the things, ways, habits, and sinfulness that need to be pruned from our lives. The Holy Spirit works in conjunction with God's word to convict us and prompt us to make these transformations. Jesus told us that to abide in Him involves abiding (stay, dwell, hang around, remain, stick around, and tarry) in His Word because it cleanses us. The Bible teaches much about prayer, the power of it, how to pray, and how God responds to our prayer, but Jesus promises us here that when His word abides in us, and we pray accordingly, when our motives are to glorify God when we are engaged in fruit-bearing work for the Kingdom and putting forth a witness to the world about Him, we can ask whatever we will, and it will be given to us:

> John 15:7. KJV *If ye abide in me, and my words abide in you, ye shall ask what ye will, and it shall be done unto you.*

Fruitlessness is a dry, unproductive place, and you can get stuck there. It's a life where one's priorities are misdirected away from God toward the material and carnal. Prayer is the anecdote for fruitlessness.

4. ABIDE IN HIS LOVE AND OBEY (John 15:9-11)

Do you remember the song "Love and Happiness" by Al Green? Well, Jesus' version of that the song would be "Love and Obedience."

> John 15:9-10: *"As the Father has loved me, so have I loved you. Now remain in my love. If you keep my commands, you will remain in my love, just as I have kept my Father's commands and remain in his love."*

JESUS HAS A SPECIAL LOVE FOR HIS OWN

God loves all of His creation, but He has a special love for His son. When we accept His Son as our Savior, we are brought into a Holy "Love Triangle." The presence of love is powerful, and it heals. On the contrary, the absence of love can do damage and create deep wounds. Some people have been unloved, under-loved, unequally loved, improperly loved, and, thus, incompletely loved. These types of dysfunctional love come from man. Jesus' love is perfect, doesn't vary or waver, and He's not stingy with it:

> 1 John 3:1: *See what great love the Father has lavished on us, that we should be called children of God! And that is what we are!*

Jesus wants His own to hang around, stay in, dwell in, tarry in, and abide in that great love. In John 14, Jesus tells us that obeying Him is an important proof of our love for Him. In John 15, He teaches about connecting to Him, Jesus tells us that He wants us to remain in His special love and just soak it up as He lavishes it on us. Obedience is part of the formula and the way to make that happen. He set the standard for us by His example of obedience to His Father.

Because of His great love for us, Jesus stands in the gap for us. He goes before us, to be present where we can't be or can't even see, doing what we are unable to do in situations we don't even know are about to happen. Jesus' great love for us combined with our love for him will compel us to walk in obedience to him.

5. ABIDE IN HIS LOVE AND LOVE OTHERS AS JESUS COMMANDED (John 15:12, 17)

THE LOVE OF JESUS

Jesus puts forth His example of laying down His life as the greatest act and ultimate expression of love. I remember as a child looking at pictures of the Thirteen Stations of the Cross which were displayed around the walls in my Sunday School class. The Stations of the Cross are part of the traditions of the Episcopal Church and the Catholic Church. It's a beautiful pictorial display of the Passion of Christ. The pictures begin with Jesus' suffering in the Garden of Gethsemane and take you through the steps of His arrest, trials, brutalization, bearing of the Cross, crucifixion, death, and burial. I studied in that Sunday School classroom for several years, and my eyes were always drawn to those images. It broke my little heart to see what Jesus went through. I couldn't understand why people were so cruel to him. Since I had been taught about the miracles He had performed, I knew he had power. But I couldn't understand why He just took his persecutors' cruelty and didn't use His powers to fight back. The Stations of the Cross drove home the point to me that Jesus suffered greatly. I later came to understand that He did it for me, and He did it because of love.

The world may not know everything about who Jesus is, but if it knows of Him, the one thing the world does know is that He was about love.

Unbelievers watch believers and are quick to call us out when they think we are not walking in love. The Love Walk or lack thereof tends to be the world's litmus test to determine if we are real Christians. Sometimes, when we speak the hard truths that Jesus has given to us just as He spoke them, they incorrectly categorize that as not showing love. People may debate and question many of Jesus' commands. They may reject His definitions of what is a sin. But most people accept that He was and is the personification of love.

The love Jesus has for us is Divine and is the highest level of love. It is a love that compels us and constrains us. It's not enough for believers to know Jesus' love and to live in it. He commands us to give His love to others. He doesn't hint, suggest, or recommend that we love one another. He commands it of us. Jesus tells us many things, but some things he comes right out and bluntly says, "I command you to do this." Loving others is one of those things He demands that we do.

Furthermore, He calls us to a very lofty, high standard of "loving" that we in our own strength are not able to pull off. He created us, knows our weaknesses, and knows that we can struggle with loving to the level of His expectations. I believe that is the reason He demands it from us.

But He will also give us the help we need to love those who are hard to love, to continue loving those who misuse our love, and to keep loving those who don't reciprocate our love. He knows the power of His love, for His love has drawing power, and when His love is displayed in us, it is able to draw people to Him.

> Ephesians 5:1-2: *Be imitators of God, therefore, as dearly loved children and live a life of love, just as Christ loved us and gave himself up for us as a fragrant offering and sacrifice to God.*

6. ABIDE IN JESUS' FRIENDSHIP (John 15:13-15)

> *"What a friend we have in Jesus, All our sins and griefs to bear! What a privilege to carry everything to God in prayer!"*

Joseph M. Scrivener wrote this beloved hymn in 1855. It tells of the friend like no other that Jesus will be to you. In John 15, Jesus describes different aspects of His friendship and lets us know there are great benefits as well as challenges that come with it. Following are the important points Jesus makes about the friendship he desires with you (John 15:13-19):

> He gave His life because of it – verse 13.
>
> Your obedience to His commandments is a requirement of the friendship - verse 14.
>
> He doesn't consider or call you a servant but calls you friend - verse 15.
>
> He has shared everything He has learned from His father - verse 15.
>
> You have been chosen and appointed by Jesus - verse 16.
>
> He is sending you out to bear eternal fruit as evidence of his friendship - verse 16.
>
> You have been called out from among the world to come into His friendship - verse 19.
>
> You may be hated and persecuted by the world because of His friendship - verse 18.

7. ABIDE IN THE TRUE VINE AND BRANCH OUT TO THE WORLD (John 15:16)

The Apostle John's life is a very dramatic example of how abiding with Christ can radically change a persons' life. John and his brother James answered Jesus' call to follow Him. They left their life's work as fishermen to become fishers of men.

Jesus gave them the nickname of "Sons of Thunder" because of their passionate tempers and fiery personalities (Mark 3:17). John walked closely with Jesus for over three years, so he saw, heard, and experienced many amazing things. He became part of Jesus' inner circle and was present at the bright shining glory of the Transfiguration and the deep sorrow of Gethsemane.

After walking with Jesus, John became very secure and confident in his knowledge of Jesus' love for him. For John, that love had become the essence of who John was and how he came to define himself. He even took to calling himself the disciple "whom Jesus loved" (John 13:23, 19:26, 21:7).

John, the Son of Thunder, was transformed into the Apostle of Love. He had witnessed the crucifixion of his beloved Savior, and as Jesus hung on the cross, Jesus asked John to care for His mother, Mary. John left a substantial mark on the world by authoring a unique book of the gospel in addition to three books of the New Testament. He also told us about the incredible vision he was given, which we know as the Book of Revelation. He became a powerful and influential leader of the early Church.

A fisherman accomplished all this with a fiery temper. John's transformative experience after being with and abiding in Christ was similar to the experience of all those disciples who had walked with Jesus and believed in Him. It will also be your experience after accepting and abiding in Him.

Like John, Jesus is calling you to come and to unite with Him on the vine. Connected to Him, He will save you, love on you, nourish you, change the way you see yourself, and transform you. He then expects the new, regenerated you to branch out to the world so that the world can see what God has done in your life. Hopefully, the witness of your transformed life will cause others to desire what you have and then lead them to accept Jesus Christ as their Savior. As we branch out to the unbelieving world, don't expect to be received by all with open arms. Jesus warns us that we can expect the same treatment He received—to be hated and persecuted. My prayer for you, dear reader, is that, like John, you will see yourself and redefine yourself by the love of Jesus Christ.

8. ABIDING AND SANCTIFICATION (John 15:1-17, 26-27)

For the believer, the journey begins with salvation by faith in Jesus Christ. We confess His name, confess our sins, and receive His Spirit. The Holy Spirit then comes to live in and indwell in us. A process begins of reorienting and redirecting "self" away from the old (sins, habits, behaviors, nature) to the new (new life and new nature). The Holy Spirit is the reorienting agent that God uses to make that happen. Another very important work of the Holy Spirit is a "maturing" ministry that is continually working in us, helping us to grow spiritually and to know the way.

The Holy Spirit empowers us to bring forth the new, the holy, and to cast off the old and the carnal. Sanctification is defined as being set apart by God, devoted to Him, empowered to do His work.

Sanctification is a believer's lifelong journey towards spiritual maturity. The Holy Spirit is the internal pilot of our sanctification journey. He convicts us and makes us know the things about ourselves that are not right, that need to be changed or cast off. Sometimes, we get caught up in the grip of sin. Sometimes, we find ourselves battling against strongholds and besetting sins. God definitely has the power and ability to give us immediate deliverance from those things. Most of us have heard dramatic testimonies of people God caused to quit drinking or drugging cold turkey. That might be your testimony. But there are other times when God does an ongoing sanctifying work in us and peels back ungodly things in us like layers on an onion. For me, I was caught up in bitterness. People knew me to be a nice person, and I was, until you crossed, hurt, or betrayed me. I could develop a quiet, lingering spirit of bitterness towards you that I would harbor, and wallow in subsequently. God had to do a work in me to remove that bitter spirit with its bitter roots. However, it was over several years before I was truly free of it.

Jesus left us a roadmap and many resources to help us to know the way so that we don't get off course along the journey. Sanctification is an identifying marker on the road and a critical component of the journey. It's the process whereby we strive for Holiness so that we can become more and more like Christ. Abiding is an important key to sanctification; the two go hand in hand with each other to do the work of transforming and reorienting us.

Both are a life-long journey and should become our lifestyle. Our old nature is always in the background, never letting go of its desire to push to the fore, take center stage, and lead us astray. We must submit and surrender daily to our Savior who delights in his role of drawing us close to him. As we abide in him, he strengthens and empowers us to make the changes and do the work that brings God glory. Grab hold to the vine with confidence and never let go.

ABIDE IN CHRIST - SUBMIT AND BE CENTERED IN HIM

Does the following describe your approach to life?

> Me, Me
> All Me
> All Me All the Time

God's pruning of us helps to channel our energies and growth away from "self" priorities and move us toward his priorities. As you abide in Christ and mature spiritually, you will experience a shift in your focus. Your approach to life will undergo a transition that may look like this:

> Me, Me
> Me, Jesus
> Jesus, Me
> Jesus, Me and Others

To be a branch that yields eternal fruit for Christ, you will have to live a life that is centered in, yielded unto, and nourished by Him.

9. Abide In Christ: What Jesus Wants You To Know About Him From John 15

He is the True Vine.

His Word will cleanse you.

He wants you to abide in Him and bear fruit for Him.

He promises that He will answer your prayers to the glory of God.

He and His Father have a special love for their own.

He wants you to abide in His love and obey Him. He has commanded you to love in the manner in which He loves.

He wants to be your friend. He has a plan for your life.

He was hated and persecuted by the world, and you will also be.

His Spirit, the Holy Spirit, will testify about Him. He wants His disciples to testify about Him.

10. ABIDING IN CHRIST: WHAT THAT LOOKS LIKE - ACCORDING TO HIM

You are connected and united to Him in an intimate relationship.

You live for Him because He lives in you, His spirit dwells in you. You see yourself as a branch off of Him.

You are in His Word to the point it is an abiding habit, and it is cleansing, pruning, and changing you.

You are shedding ungodly habits and things that were clinging to you, and you now cling to Him.

You strive to have the mind of Christ and be conformed to His image. You display the character of Christ to the world.

You now display more fruit of the spirit than the fruit of the flesh and carnality.

You have tried doing it on your own, apart from Him, have failed and are now clinging to Him.

You pray about everything in accordance with His Word, seeking His will, worrying about nothing.

You trust and believe His promise that He hears your prayers and will answer them.

You are discovering the depth of His love for you, and your relationship with Him is grounded in that love.

You know that Jesus is your example in all things and strive to follow His examples.

You strive to obey all of His commands.

You strive to honor His command to love your brethren with the unique love of Jesus Christ.

You know you have access to His joy, which He has given you. It completes you and is a source of strength to you.

You realize you are a chosen, appointed vessel and that Jesus is your friend.

You have come to understand what your position is in Christ and desire to bear good, lasting fruit for His Kingdom.

11. ABIDE IN CHRIST: WHAT NOT ABIDING IN CHRIST LOOKS LIKE

You HAVE NOT received Christ in your heart as Lord and Savior, or you have done that, but you are in a marginal, backslidden, or fallen away relationship with Him.

You DO NOT live for Him but everything and everyone but Him. He is pretty much an afterthought, if that, in what you do and say. You can't see yourself as a branch off of Him. Or you tried living for Him once or even a few times but can't seem to get it right.

You are NOT in His Word, or if so, not in any disciplined or habitual way. Thus, it has NOT cleansed or changed you. Or you have tried studying the Bible but don't really understand it or know how to apply it to your life and have given up on trying.

You HAVE NOT recognized the ungodly things and habits that are clinging to you, and if you have you have been unable to shed them. Yet you still cling to everyone and everything except the one who is able to set you free.

You DO NOT know what the mind of Christ means or are confused about it. You feel that what you think and what you feel is the successful way to navigate in this life and are led by that.

You DO NOT display more fruit of the spirit than the fruit of the flesh and may even be flat out carnal.

You CONTINUE trying to do it on your own, apart from Him, despite failure and yet CONTINUE clinging to worldly people, things, and strategies that will fail you.

You DO NOT pray about everything or possibly anything, or when you pray, it is in contradiction to his Word. You DO NOT seek his will before acting, and you worry about everything.

You DO NOT trust and believe His promise that He hears your prayers and are unsure if He will answer them.

You HAVE NOT discovered the depth of his love for you and DO NOT have a relationship with Him grounded in that love.

You DO NOT know that Jesus is your example in all things and follow everyone's example but His.

You DO NOT strive to obey His commands.

You DO NOT strive to honor His command to love your brethren with the unique love of Jesus Christ. You may even consider acting in love as a weakness.

You DO NOT know you have access to His joy, which He has given you. Thus, you feel incomplete, sad, depressed, and are in a weakened state.

You DO NOT realize you are a chosen, appointed vessel nor realize what a friend you have in Jesus.

You DO NOT understand what your position is in Christ nor desire to bear good, lasting fruit for His Kingdom.

JESUS PRAYED FOR YOU TO KNOW THE WAY – JOHN 17

I remember the first time I read Jesus' High Priestly Prayer in John 17 with understanding, and I really "got it." It brought me to tears as I read that prayer and realized that Jesus was actually praying for me. Yes, that's right; over 2,000 years ago, Jesus stood on earth, reached across time, and prayed to God his Father about me. That I would be one with the body of Christ - his Church - just as he was one with God, thereby presenting a powerful witness to the world about him.

> *John 17 Living Bible (TLB)*
>
> *18 As you sent me into the world, I am sending them into the world, 19 and I consecrate myself to meet their need for growth in truth and holiness.*
>
> *20 "I am not praying for these alone but also for the future believers who will come to me*
>
> *because of the testimony of these. 21 My prayer for all of them is that they will be of one heart and mind, just as you and I are, Father—that just as you are in me and I am in you, so they will be in us, and the world will believe you sent me.*
>
> *22 "I have given them the glory you gave me—the glorious unity of being one, as we are— 23 I in them and you in me, all being perfected into one— so that the world will know you sent me and will understand that you love them as much as you love me. 24 Father, I want them with me—these you've given me—so that they can see my glory. You gave me the glory because you loved me before the world began!*
>
> *25 "O righteous Father, the world doesn't know you, but I do; and these disciples know you sent me. 26 And I have revealed you to them and will keep on revealing you so that the mighty love you have for me may be in them, and I in them."*

Did you see it? Jesus prayed for you—verse 20! For your protection and spiritual growth. He prayed that you would have a fruitful life filled and overflowing with his love. He prayed for a life that results in a compelling witness of his love for the world. That you are forever connected to Him and connected to other believers in the Body of Christ. He has given us His life, His Spirit, His divine resources and this magnificent prayer so that we will always be able to know the way to Him.

> 2 Peter 1:3: *His divine power has given us everything we need for a godly life through our knowledge of him who called us by his own glory and goodness.*

Jesus, oh thou son of David, have mercy on us. Remove not your hand from us and keep us forever in the way.

God Will Send People into Your Life to Help Show You the Way

> 1 Corinthians 11:1: "Follow my example as I follow the example of Christ."

We have studied Jesus' precious words in John 14 & 15 and His beautiful prayer in John 17. He gave us a long list of Spiritual tools in these chapters.

These powerful tools will help ensure that we will always be able to find the way to Him, abide in Him, and abide in His love. In John 17, Jesus reaches across time and seals it all with an extraordinary prayer for our protection, unity, and witness to the world. Another very significant way that God helps us always to know that "the way" is that He sends people into our lives that help guide us.

One of the ways in which God has so richly blessed me is by giving me a tremendous cloud of Godly people that He has faithfully placed in my life everywhere my feet have tread. I especially thank Him for the women who have blessed my life with their examples and teaching, and I want to recognize them. Many amazing Godly women have prayed for me, with me, and have helped me to know what "The Walk" looks like. The women who have impacted my Christian development the most are the ones I call "Lynette's Cloud." The book of Hebrews eloquently speaks about a great cloud of witnesses in the following passage:

> Hebrews 12:1: *Therefore, since we are surrounded by such a great cloud of witnesses, let us throw off everything that hinders and the sin that so easily entangles. And let us run with perseverance the race marked out for us.*

LYNETTE'S CLOUD

My cloud begins with my mother, Elise Jackson Grant, my Aunt Ina Johnson Brown, and my sister/cousins - Antinetta Vanderhost and Alice Brown Poole. I spoke about these women in my dedication at the beginning of this book. There are several others that I would like to acknowledge as well.

I want to recognize my sweet spirited mother-in-law, Magnolia Love, a dedicated Church Servant who served her Church for many years. She had the gifts of love and patience and passed them on to her children. She also had the gift of hospitality and much of what I know about hosting guests in my home, I learned from her.

Have you ever had someone show up in your life and bless you so richly that it almost blew you away? And you know there was no other possible explanation for their presence in your life but that they were sent to you by God. For me, that would be Anne Hitchcock, sent by God to help us raise our two sons and to help me strengthen my faith. In that season of my life, I was a young, stressed out, working professional woman. Anne Hitchcock came into my home every day when our youngest son Reggie, was four years old and babysat our two sons until Reggie went to middle school. I will forever be grateful for all that she did for our family and for the impact she had on the development of my faith.

From the time that I was three until age nine, my family lived in Camden, New Jersey. Thank you, God, for those two Spiritual giants: Arthuree Evans and Cousin Augusta Francis, that you placed in our lives to help my mother. My mother had separated from my father and had moved from Chicago to Camden, NJ, with three small children in tow. Those two cousins took my mother and family under their wings with open arms. "Aunt" Arthuree was one of the first women I was exposed to who was that model of the dedicated, hard-working Church Servant.

She was also very bright and a natural leader. I have often thought that if she had lived in the time of opportunities available to women today, she would probably be running a Fortune 500 company or something of that magnitude.

From age 9-17, I lived in Mt. Pleasant, SC, in the segregated South amongst a very large clan of relatives from my mothers' side of the family—the Germans and the Johnsons. My family's roots go back to slavery in that area. I am thankful for the influence of many people from that place and time, but especially for the spiritual influence of Mrs. Virginia Singleton, Mrs. Margaret Lesene, and my precious cousins Janie Howard, Sarah Days, Lucille Potter, Hilda Bodkin, Dot Dupree, Mabel Coakley, TeeDee Johnson, Harriett Johnson and Stella German-Green.

These women have never stopped praying for me and encouraging me, and they continue to do so even until this day. I know that those who have gone on to glory are watching over me from heaven. A familiar African-proverb says it takes a whole village to raise a child. I can say that I have truly had the "village raising" experience.

Also, from my time spent in Mt. Pleasant, SC, I thank God for my "crew." Starting in elementary and middle school, I formed bonds with Nancy Horry Dede, Bernice Lesene Huell, Margaret Lesene Cochran, Rita Ascue Worthy, Claudia Brown, and Karen McNeil. All of us were all raised alike – in the Church. Each time I get to reconnect with them, I marvel at and thank God for how He has kept all of us in the faith. Additionally, I see that our belief in God has not faltered but has been strengthened by life's challenges. No matter where I go in life, I know that these ladies love me, will pray for me, and will always have my back.

Cheryl Duboise and Gestine Brown joined Victory Christian Center Church in Charlotte, NC, the same time that I did. We went through New Members' Training classes together and connected as sisters in Christ. No matter how frequently or infrequently we speak to one another, that connection remains. Also, while I was living in Charlotte, Anne Dames was a source of inspiration to me. I continue to be inspired by Anne's powerful evangelistic example of going into people's homes to do Bible studies. She probably doesn't even realize the impact she has had on me.

I had two brothers; I was the baby and the only girl. I always wanted a sister and was always looking for a sister. I found one in Lillian Huger. Not just a sister but a spiritual sister. We both were working for a company in Concord, NC, and discovered we were from the same hometown of Mt. Pleasant, SC. Like most of us raised at that time, and place, she too, was raised in the Church. Lillian never fails to bring laughter with her. In addition to getting a humorous take on things from her, I can always count on getting that spiritual perspective with her advice.

From my time living in Pinehurst, NC, I am thankful for my Bible Study Fellowship (BSF) buddies, Ms. Vivian Kelly, and Ms. Sadie Smalls. For two years, we took the thirty-five-minute weekly drive to Fayetteville, NC, to participate in BSF. Their fellowship and friendship to me were priceless.

When I lived in Colorado Springs Co, God sent Clara Barksdale, Jackie Lee, Bernice Cowart; Jeanine Moore; Maryanne Townsend; Shanaz Jones; and Alva Wilson as lights in my life to help me grow in Him and to show me the beauty of His magnificent creation in Colorado Springs and the state of Colorado. You talk about women who really loved The Lord! With Sister Clara Barksdale, I know I can always depend on her to give me straight-up Godly advice that is not going to deviate one iota from God's Word.

When I moved to Sacramento, CA, God really "showed out." I moved there not knowing one person, but God sent me: Macia Fuller, Gloria Hester; Claudia West; Cecilia Lawson; Barbara Jenkins; and Brenda Dilliard. These women took me under their wings, loved on me, and blessed me with their friendship. God also sent the amazing Vanessa Logan into my life, with whom my husband

and I worked in the Marriage Enrichment Ministry at St. Paul's Missionary Baptist Church.

When we moved to Raleigh, NC, the ever-faithful God caused my life to intersect with Dr. Sherri Arnold Graham, Deacon Charlotte Humphrey, Jackie McLamb, and Dorothy Gillis Branch. As God had done many times before, he caused my Spirit to connect with these Godly women, resulting in learning and growth for me. In Raleigh, I have met and worked in Ministries with Audrey Burnette, Armequin Mann, Allie Bynum, Josie Greene, Ernestine Lavenhouse, Mary Teasley, and Debra Hooper. Their friendship has been one of the blessings that I have received while serving.

Other women whom God has included in my cloud are my Richmond, VA buddies: Sylvia Smith, Berna Redmond, Rose Johnson, Belinda Johnson, and Rose Studivant. I was coming from a very sheltered background, was young in my marriage, and was just starting my professional career when I moved to Richmond. "What would I have done with myself in Richmond without these ladies?"

I would also like to acknowledge my sisters in law, Glo Mercer, and Debra Price. I have been family with these ladies for over 45 years.

The Women of Bible Study Fellowship

BSF Bible Study Fellowship is an in-depth, interdenominational Bible study with classes across America and throughout the world. I have participated in this wonderful Bible Study in four states and six cities and have found it to be consistently excellent. I spent 12 years studying with this ministry and was a Discussion Group Leader for eight of those years. BSF does an in-depth, line-by-line, and word-by-word study of the Bible that changed my life. When you get into the Word of God in any depth, the Word does what the Word does—it transforms you. One of the many things about BSF that blesses you so is the fellowship with other women. To hear women in those discussion groups speak freely about their love for the Lord, and their spiritual journeys helped me on so many levels. Every week, the women in the small groups would pray for each other, plus the leaders would join together twice each week, getting on their knees to pray for the women and the needs of the BSF ministry. Hearing praise reports regarding answers to those prayers helped to cement my belief in the power of prayer, increased my boldness about going before the throne of grace, and built up my confidence that I would freely receive God's mercy and grace in my time of need.

The Women of Shepherds Heart Ministry, Raleigh, NC

My husband and I moved to Raleigh, NC, in 2011. Just before we received news that we would be relocating there, my wonderful friend, Ceceila Lawson, had given me a book for my birthday that mentioned a women's prison ministry in Raleigh. After we moved to Raleigh, I contacted this powerful ministry and started serving as a Group Leader. When I arrived in Raleigh in 2011, I was somewhat at loose ends, and Shepherd's Heart Ministry was part of the thread that God used to help me tie up my loose ends. Once again, I found myself in the midst of women who loved and served the Lord wholeheartedly. In addition to facilitating Bible Study for women in prison every Wednesday night, I was now among 20+ leaders who were prayer warriors lifting up each other's needs before God on an ongoing basis. An added blessing was that I got to know the Teaching Leader of this ministry, the awesome Linda Horton, whose anointed teaching and Godly example of her life has blessed me beyond measure.

As you can see, my "Cloud" has been enormous, and I have been blessed to have lived a life that has been covered in prayer by many Godly people, mostly women. Whatever the season, need or place,

God has been so faithful in sending into my life the angel that I needed for that time. I honor all of these women and the scores of other unnamed women like them who rarely receive accolades for who they are and what they do. These women are not famous, nor do they seek recognition. They quietly go about their lives, working diligently in their Churches, serving, teaching, mentoring, praying, doing ministry outreach, and sharing the gospel. Many Churches and Christian organizations would have withered long ago without such women (and men) who have willingly been God's hands and feet in the earth realm.

In Hebrews 10 & 11, we are given the examples of saints and patriarchs of great faith whose lives provide a "cloud of witnesses" that surround us and encourage us to run on. In addition to giving me that "cloud" of great men and women of the Bible to encourage me, God gave me my very own cast of spiritual characters in the story of my life. I could never claim not to know who I was to be as a Christian Woman. God put far too many Godly women in my life for me to ever be confused about what that is supposed to look like. These women helped to show me the way.

I have read dedications and acknowledgments in other books that went on and on naming people that I did not know, causing me to glaze over those sections. Dear readers, I hope it was not too boring for you to be reading the names of women that you don't know personally. As you read about these women in my life, it has probably caused you to think about the people in your life, like the ones I mentioned who have blessed you. Take a few minutes to think about these people in your life. Take a minute to thank God for them. Take the time to thank them for yourselves.

Remember that one important way to thank them is by giving out to others what you have received from them and by helping to show others the way.

LYNETTE'S CLOUD

Part 1:
STUDY QUESTIONS

Jesus Leaves a Roadmap in The Gospel of John Pointing the Way

1. **Jesus Tells Us Not to Let Our Hearts Be Troubled and to Believe**

   (Read John 13, 14:1-4).

   Briefly summarize what happened in John 13.

   ....
   ....
   ....
   ....

   In John 13-17, Jesus has gathered His disciples into His presence for some very intimate time with Him. What can we expect to happen when we are in the presence of the Lord?

   ....
   ....
   ....
   ....

Jesus told us not to let our hearts be troubled. But trouble does come in this life. What do you get out of these chapters that can help you to protect your heart from being troubled when trouble comes?

....
....
....

1.2 Jesus is the only way to God and is truth and life

(Read John 14:5-6).

....
....
....

Why do you think that Thomas and the other disciples were so confused about what Jesus was saying?

....
....
....

What should you do if you are confused about a doctrine, principle, or foundational Christian truth?

....
....
....

Jesus told us that He is the only way to God, but other faiths take issue with this foundational Christian doctrine, and many reject it. Ecumenicalism is defined as the promoting of cooperation, understanding, and unity among different world religions. How should Christians manage the tension between ecumenicalism, interfaith initiatives, and their Christian beliefs?

....
....
....
....

Read John 18:28-38 and Matthew 27:19.

....
....
....
....

What is your assessment of how Pilate handled this situation? Do you see Pilate-like similarities in how people handle things today?

....
....
....
....

The world often levels charges of lack of compassion and lack of love when Christians take an unpopular stand based on God's truths. How should Christians manage the tension between standing on God's truths versus doing it in love and showing compassion?

....
....
....

How do you become grounded in God's truths so that you can withstand the cultural forces of changing moral standards in today's world? (Read John 11:1-44).

....
....
....

Summarize what happened. How does Jesus prove in this passage that He is Life?

....
....
....

1.3 Jesus and God are One (Read John 14:7-11).

....
....
....

Jesus and God are One. How would you explain this oneness to someone?

....
....
....
....

What do you think about the way and the timing of how Nicodemus approached Jesus?

....
....
....
....

Describe the Ministry of Regeneration that Jesus said begins with being born again of water and the Spirit.

....
....
....
....

From John 14:7-11, identify 5 key points Jesus makes that helps us to believe that He and God are One.

....
....
....
....

1.4 Jesus' Followers Will do Great Works (Read John 14:12).

What is the first and most important work that Jesus desires of us?

....
....
....

What is the greatest work that Jesus did for us?

....
....
....

What is the greatest work that believers are called to?

(Read 1 Corinthians 12).

....
....
....

What is the role of the Holy Spirit in the identification and use of a believer's gifts and talents?

(Read Exodus 31:1-11 and Exodus 35: 30-36:1).

....
....
....

List all the gifts, talents, and skills God gave to the workers building His Tabernacle.

....
....
....
....

List your gifts and talents. Which of these do you feel are anointed by God? How are you using them?

....
....
....
....

1.5 Jesus' Name has Power (Read John 14:13-14).

God exalted Jesus' name to the highest, above all names. List some of the ways that believers can exalt Jesus' name.

....
....
....

List some examples of praying in the name of Jesus incorrectly.

....
....
....

The apostles were the first ones to pray in Jesus' name, and they did it freely, frequently, and confidently. What were they asking for as they prayed in Jesus' name in the following New Testament scriptures?

....
....
....
....

1 Cor. 6:11

....
....
....
....

Acts 3:5-7, 16

....
....
....

Acts 16:17-19

....
....
....

Acts 9:27-28

....
....
....

1 Cor 1:10

....
....
....
....

1 Cor. 5:3

....
....
....
....

Ephesians 5:20

....
....
....
....

James 5:14

....
....
....
....

The Prosperity Gospel

....
....
....
....

The Prosperity Gospel is defined as a modern version or, according to some, perversion of the Gospel according to which the full blessings of God are available to those who approach Him in faith and obedience and include wealth, health, and power (Collins English Dictionary - Complete & Unabridged 2012 Digital Edition).

....
....
....
....

a. How do you reconcile "the prosperity gospel" with Jesus' promise that we can ask Him for anything in His name, and He will do it?

....
....
....

b. How is the way the apostles are praying in the name of Jesus in the scriptures above different from how "the prosperity gospel" might promote praying in Jesus' name?

....
....
....

1.6 Jesus Says that Loving Him Means Obeying Him

What key points does Jesus make in the following verses?

....
....
....
....

John 14:15

....
....
....
....

John14:21

....
....
....
....

John 14:23-24

....
....
....

John 14:31

....
....
....

What do you learn from these verses and this section of the book about the obedience Jesus' desires of you?

....
....
....
....

Give an example of how:

....
....
....
....

a. A Christian's obedience provides a witness to the world about his or her love for Jesus.

....
....
....

b. A Christian's disobedience is a witness to the world about the level of his or her love for Jesus and the state of his or her relationship with Him.

....
....
....

1.7 Jesus Gives Us the Promise of The Holy Spirit Who Will Help to Show Us the Way (Read John 14: 16-17).

....
....
....
....

From what Jesus says in these verses, how will the role of the Holy Spirit in the life of His followers differ from the role of the Holy Spirit in the Old Testament?

(See Acts 2: 1-13).

....
....
....
....

What denomination do you belong to, and what is its style of worship? What does it believe about the Holy Spirit's role in worship?

....
....
....

What do you know about The Holy Spirit?

....
....
....

How would you rate your level of knowledge about Him on a scale of 1-10 (10 being highest)?

....
....
....
....

What confusion do you have about The Holy Spirit?

....
....
....
....

Have you ever been in a charismatic, spirit-filled worship service and felt as if you were "missing the boat?"

....
....
....
....

Have you ever been criticized or ridiculed because people felt that you were either too dry or too over the top in your worship?

....
....
....
....

The Holy Spirit at Creation (Read Genesis 1).

From Genesis 1, can you see the Holy Spirit's role in Creation? What are your thoughts about His role? (See Genesis 1:2 and Genesis 1:26-27).

....
....
....

In what ways do you need to experience the creative powers of the Holy Spirit in your life today?

....
....
....

The Holy Spirit and the People in the Old Testament

What is the role of the Holy Spirit and or what do you learn about Him in the following scriptures?

....
....
....

Moses: Numbers 11:16-17, Numbers 11:25-29

....
....
....

Joshua: Numbers 27:18-20, Deuteronomy 34:9

....
....
....

Gideon: Judges 6:33-35

....
....
....

Sampson: Judges 14:5-6

....
....
....

Saul: 1 Samuel 10: 9-11

....
....
....

David: 1 Samuel 16: 10-13 | 2 Samuel 23:1-2 | 1 Chronicles 28:11-12

....
....
....

Joseph: Genesis 41:37-39

....
....
....

The Holy Spirit and the Earthly Ministry of Jesus

What is the role of the Holy Spirit and or what do you learn about Him in the following scriptures?

....
....
....

Acts 10:38

....
....
....

Matthew 1:18-21

....
....
....

Matthew 3:16-17

....
....
....

Matthew 4:1

....
....
....

Luke 4:14-15

....
....
....

Romans 8:11

....
....
....

Read John 14:16-17; 14:26; 15:26; 16:7-15.

List all the key points Jesus teaches us about the Holy Spirit and His role in a believer's life.

....
....
....

1.8 Jesus Has Given Us His Peace (Read John 14:27).

....
....
....

Jesus is our example in all things, and He gave us his example of how to operate in peace while under the most conflict-laden, challenging, and brutal circumstances.

....
....
....

What do you learn from His example that you can use in your life to help you operate in His peace?

....
....
....
....

What advice would you give someone to help them sustain his or her sense of inner calm while in the midst of chaotic, troubling, or turbulent circumstances?

....
....
....
....

How does the peace of Jesus Christ differ from that which the world proclaims as peace?

....
....
....
....

How does being in God's will impact our sense of peace or lack of peace?

....
....
....
....

In what way(s) might you currently be leaving the doors of your life open to peace stealers?

....
....
....

What do the following scriptures say about peace?

....
....
....

1 Corinthians 14:33

....
....
....

Hebrews 12:14

....
....
....

Colossians 3:15

....
....
....

Mark 4:39

....
....
....

Galatians 5:22

....
....
....

Matthew 11:28-30

....
....
....

Romans 8:6

....
....
....

Isaiah 26:3

....
....
....

Isaiah 54:10

....
....
....

Romans 14:17-19

....
....
....

Romans 12:17

....
....
....
....

Psalm 37:37

....
....
....
....

1.9 Jesus Gave Us the John 14 Roadmap.

Summarize the John 14 Roadmap that helps us to know the way to Christ.

....
....
....
....

Part 2:
STUDY QUESTIONS

JESUS INVITES YOU TO ABIDE IN HIM AND LET HIS SPIRIT DWELL IN YOU TO SHOW YOU THE WAY

Abide in Jesus the True Vine (Read John 15:1).

....
....
....
....

How does Jesus describe the relationship He desires with us in this passage?

....
....
....
....

How are we transformed by it?

....
....
....
....

Jesus starts John 15 with an "I am" statement declaring himself to be the True Vine. What is the symbolism and significance of the Vine and the True Vine?

....
....
....
....

What are some of the parallels between a grapevine and a believer's relationship with Jesus?

....
....
....
....

What happens when we are not fully connected to Jesus or do not remain so?

....
....
....

2.1 & 2.2 Abide in Christ to be Purposeful, Fruitful and a Reflection of His Character (Read John 15: 2-6, 8).

....
....
....
....

Jesus says in John 15:2..."every branch that does bear fruit he prunes so that it will be even more fruitful."

....
....
....
....

What is God's purpose for pruning believers, and what methods does He use?

....
....
....
....

What does fruitlessness look like in a believer and what are some of its causes? What are some of the consequences of fruitlessness?

....
....
....
....

List the fruits of the Spirit and/or fruits of the flesh from the following passages and share what the scriptures say about them.

....
....
....
....

Galatians 5: 22-23

....
....
....
....

Galatians 5:19-21

....
....
....

Philippians 2:1-5

....
....
....

How is one able to successfully show the character and mindset of Christ when handling the challenge of messy, manipulative, rude, selfish, or dysfunctional people?

....
....
....

Give some examples of strongholds and besetting sins with which believers might struggle.

....
....
....

2.3 Abide in His Word and Pray (Read John 15:7, 16).

....
....
....

Give some examples of things and situations in our lives that have the potential to weaken a believer's connection to Christ.

....
....
....

How does / can sin separate us from God?

....
....
....

Read Ephesians 6:10-18.

Which of the two weapons of warfare from this passage does Jesus speaks about in John 15:7.

....
....
....

Give examples of warfare situations when you would need to put these weapons into action.

....
....
....

2.4 Abide in His Love and Obey (Read John 15:9-11).

What does Jesus say about the connection between love and obedience?

....
....
....
....

Why do you think Jesus expressed so strongly (commanded) that we love as He loves?

....
....
....
....

How would you describe the Love of Jesus Christ?

....
....
....
....

Share a time that you have experienced His love in a special way.

....
....
....
....

John and all the disciples experienced the transformative Love of Jesus Christ. What in your life needs to be transformed by the Love of Jesus?

....
....
....
....

How does a believer give out hard truths to someone while doing it in love? Give an example of how you would do that.

....
....
....
....

2.5 Abide in His Love and Love Others as Jesus Commanded (Read John 15:12, 17).

....
....
....
....

Make a list of all the ways that Jesus sacrificed and suffered because of His love for us.

....
....
....

Who might God be calling you to make a sacrifice(s) for during this season of your life?

....
....
....

When dealing with and witnessing to nonbelievers, would you say you lead with love or judgment?

....
....
....

Jesus demanded that we operate at a very lofty standard of loving. How might you be struggling to live up to that standard?

....
....
....

2.6 Abide in Jesus' Friendship—Beneficial and Challenging Aspects of Friendship with Jesus:

(Read John 15:13-19).

> He gave His life because of it (verse 13).
>
> Your obedience to His commandments is a requirement of the friendship (verse 14).
>
> He doesn't consider or call you a servant but calls you a friend (verse 15).

> He has shared everything He has learned from His Father (verse 15).
>
> You have been chosen and appointed by Jesus (verse 16).
>
> He is sending you out to bear eternal fruit as evidence of His friendship (verse 16).
>
> You have been called out from among the world to come into His friendship (verse 19).
>
> You may be hated and persecuted by the world because of His friendship (verse 18).

Which of the above points / statements have blessed you the most?

....
....
....

Which of the above statements are the most challenging for you?

....
....
....

2.7 Abide in the True Vine and Branch out to the World (Read John 15:16).

....
....
....

Find examples in the Bible of people who were transformed by the love of Jesus Christ as they hung out with Him.

....
....
....
....
....

How secure would you say you are in the knowledge that Jesus truly loves you?

....
....
....
....

How has walking with and abiding in Jesus' love changed the way you see yourself?

....
....
....
....

2.8 ABIDING AND SANCTIFICATION (Read John 15: 1-17, 26-27).

....
....
....
....

How would you explain Sanctification to someone?

....
....
....

What is the Holy Spirit's role in Sanctification?

....
....
....

How does the process of Sanctification support a believer's ability to abide in Christ?

....
....
....

Give some examples of the types of strongholds and besetting sins with which believers might Struggle.

....
....
....

2.9 Abide in Christ: What Jesus Wants You to Know About Him from John 15

....
....
....

> He is the True Vine.
>
> His Word will cleanse you.
>
> He wants you to abide in Him and bear fruit for Him.
>
> He promises that He will answer your prayers to the Glory of God.
>
> He and His Father have a special love for their own.
>
> He wants you to abide in His love and obey Him.
>
> He has commanded you to love the way He loves.
>
> He wants to be your friend.
>
> He has a plan for your life.
>
> He was hated and persecuted by the world, and you will also be.
>
> His Spirit, the Holy Spirit will testify about Him.
>
> He wants His disciples to testify about Him.

....
....
....
....

What would you add to this list?

....
....
....
....
....

For which of the items on the above list do you desire to be strengthened?

....
....
....
....

2. 10 Abiding in Christ: What that Looks Like— According to Him

....
....
....
....

You are connected and united to Him in an intimate relationship.

....
....
....
....

You live for Him because He lives in you, His Spirit dwells in you. You see yourself as a branch off of Him.

....
....
....
....

You are in His Word to the point it is an abiding habit, and it is cleansing, pruning, and changing you.

....
....
....
....

You are shedding ungodly habits and things that were clinging to you, and you now cling to Him.

....
....
....
....

You strive to have the mind of Christ and be conformed to his image. You display the character of Christ to the world.

....
....
....
....

You now display more fruit of the Spirit than the fruit of the flesh and carnality.

....
....
....
....

You have tried doing it on your own, apart from Him, have failed, and are now clinging to Him.

You pray about everything in accordance with His Word, seeking His will, worrying about nothing.

....
....
....

You trust and believe His promise that He hears your prayers and will answer them.

....
....
....

You are discovering the depth of His love for you, and your relationship with Him is grounded in that love.

....
....
....

You know that Jesus is your example in all things and strive to follow His examples.

....
....
....

You strive to obey all of His commands.

....
....
....

You strive to honor His command to love your brethren with the unique love of Jesus Christ.

....
....
....

You know you have access to His joy, which He has given you. It completes you and is a source of strength to you.

....
....
....

You realize you are a chosen, appointed vessel and that Jesus is your friend.

....
....
....

You have come to understand what your position is in Christ and desire to bear good, lasting fruit for His Kingdom.

....
....
....

2.11 Abide in Christ: What Not Abiding in Christ Looks Like

....
....
....
....
....

You HAVE NOT received Christ in your heart as Lord and Savior, or you have done that, but you are in a marginal, backslidden, or fallen away relationship with Him.

....
....
....
....
....

You DO NOT live for Him but everything and everyone but him. He is pretty much an afterthought, if that, in what you do and say. You cannot see yourself as a branch off of Him, or you tried living for Him once or even a few times but cannot seem to get it right.

....
....
....
....
....

You are NOT in His Word, or if so, not in any disciplined or habitual way. Thus, it has NOT cleansed or changed you. Alternatively, you have tried studying the Bible but do not understand it or know how to apply it to your life and have given up on trying.

....
....
....
....

You HAVE NOT recognized the ungodly things and habits that are clinging to you, and if you have, you have been unable to shed them. You still cling to everyone and everything except the One who can set you free.

....
....
....
....

You DO NOT know what the mind of Christ means or are confused about it. You feel that what you think and what you feel is the successful way to navigate in this life and are led by that.

....
....
....

You DO NOT display more fruit of the Spirit than the fruit of the flesh and may even be flat out carnal.

....
....
....

You CONTINUE trying to do it on your own, apart from Him, despite failure and yet CONTINUE clinging to worldly people, things, and strategies that will fail you.

....
....
....

You DO NOT pray about everything or possibly anything or when you pray; it is in contradiction to His Word. You DO NOT seek his will before acting, and you worry about everything.

....
....
....

You DO NOT trust and believe his promise that He hears your prayers and are unsure if He will answer them.

....
....
....

You HAVE NOT discovered the depth of His love for you and DO NOT have a relationship with Him grounded in that love.

....
....
....
....

You DO NOT know that Jesus is your example in all things and follow everyone's example but His.

....
....
....
....

You DO NOT strive to obey His commands.

....
....
....
....

You DO NOT strive to honor His command to love your brethren with the unique love of Jesus Christ. You may even consider acting in love as a weakness.

....
....
....
....

You DO NOT know you have access to his joy, which He has given you. Thus you feel incomplete, sad, depressed, and are in a weakened state.

....
....
....
....

You DO NOT realize you are a chosen, appointed vessel nor realize what a friend you have in Jesus.

....
....
....
....

You DO NOT understand what your position is in Christ nor desire to bear good, lasting fruit for His Kingdom.

....
....
....
....

Would Jesus say you are abiding in Him or not abiding in Him?

....
....
....

Which items from the abiding /not abiding lists stand out to you, and why?

....
....
....
....

Pick two or three items from the above lists that you would like to grow in so that you can abide more closely with Jesus. What do you plan to do to make that happen?

....
....
....
....

Jesus Prayed for You to Know the Way (Read John 17).

....
....
....
....

Would you say you are a source of unity or discord in the Body of Christ (your church)?

....
....
....
....

Write a short prayer. Thank Jesus for all He has done for you. Thank Him for this wonderful prayer that He prayed for you. Ask Him to show you how to bring unity to the Church and Christian Organizations to which you belong.

....
....
....
....
....

www.ingramcontent.com/pod-product-compliance
Lightning Source LLC
Chambersburg PA
CBHW021953290426
44108CB00012B/1048